GREEN BERETS

GREEN BERETS

Unconventional Warriors

Hans Halberstadt

Presidio Press ★ Novato, California
THE PRESIDIO POWER SERIES
LANDPOWER ★3002

Published by Presidio Press
31 Pamaron Way, Novato CA 94949

LIBRARY OF CONGRESS
Library of Congress Cataloging-in-Publication Data

Halberstadt, Hans.
  Green Berets: unconventional warriors/text and photographs by Hans Halberstadt.
    p.   cm.—(The Presidio power series. Landpower; #3002)
  ISBN 0-89141-280-8:
  1. United States.   Army.   Special Forces.   I. Title.   II. Series: Presidio power series.
Landpower book; #3002.
UA34.S64H35   1988   87–30264
356'.167'0973—dc 19   CIP

Printed in the United States of America

Dedication

Sgt. Conling Chen
3rd Battalion, 12th Special Forces Group
(Airborne)

Units take casualties in times of conflict; they expect them and accept them with regret and realism; it is part of the game. Once in a while, though, they suffer losses for which they are not prepared. Sergeant Chen was one of these.

Chen was an interesting guy, one of the hard-core members of 3rd of the 12th. Favorite jump-master, veteran of the British Army, fluent in several languages. He was not, however, a graduate of the Q course, and that means he wasn't (in the official and traditional sense) an official member of SF, a Green Beret. He was not an American citizen until just before he was killed. His family, merchants and business people in Singapore, were confused and opposed to his commitment to SF. But he lived and breathed Special Forces, and was personally committed to becoming a full member of the organization and joining an A team. He changed his citizenship, was getting his security clearance, and was almost good to go. You can be part of the unit without the tab, but you can't be on a team. Sergeant Chen wanted to be on a team. He wanted the tab more than anything.

He was typical of the kind of guy who fits into SF and is happy there; he was intense. He maxed every PT test he ever took. The good ones are like that; they all operate at about 150 percent efficiency and commitment. They don't complain. They don't seem to need to sleep; when they eat or drink or party, they do it with full commitment and intensity. The best party you will *ever* attend is an SF party.

Chen was in a car wreck and he died. The unit was his home in life, and the unit took care of him when he died. His commander and his other friends went to the hospital, made all the arrangements, met the family at the airport; it was a big deal. The commander lost a lot of friends in war and peace, but he cried. They all did.

The memorial service was tough. The chaplain is a legend in SF; he's been in it since 1952. He's said good-bye to a lot of young troopers. He knows about life and death, having seen a lot of both. But the chaplain nearly didn't get through the service, either. There was something special about Chen that everybody depended on, even the chaplain. He had tapped them all out the door, even without the tab from the Q course.

So the chaplain said what he could say, and when he was done, he said that the one thing Chen had always wanted was that little tab with "SPECIAL FORCES" on it, and although he had never been able to qualify for it by attending the Q course, he had earned it a harder way, from within the unit. The chaplain said the unit decided that Chen was as qualified for it as anybody ever was. And he took a tab and placed it on Sergeant Chen's beret on the altar. Then they really cried.

Acknowledgments

This book has been one of my most interesting and challenging projects. It would never have happened without the intense interest and support of several people, and several organizations, who decided to sponsor the book. While the military generally gets a lot of flack for its information effort, I must say that the cooperation and assistance we got on this book was tremendous. And Connie Smith from Sixth Army Public Affairs is my candidate for Angel of the Year. Connie balanced the needs of the Army and the needs of the public, making sure that I had a chance to tell the story of the men and the units, while at the same time protecting their interests and security.

The Department of Defense, Forces Command, and Sixth Army, Special Operations Command (the legendary SOCOM) and the John Fitzgerald Kennedy Special Warfare Center have all been cooperative, candid, open, and fair; all they asked was fair treatment in print. In return, they helped me see and do far more than I expected. I hope they're satisfied with the result.

I also got great support from two other public relations shops, both at Fort Bragg: SOCOM, where my amigo, Bill Gerhards, and his partners in crime hang out; and right across the parking lot, SWC. A salute to Dr. Sandler, the SF historian; Jerry Steelman; Colonel Potter; and Fred Fuller for their work and insights.

Two units, one active duty, one reserve, provided the foundation for the contemporary part of this book: 1st Battalion, 7th Special Forces Group (Airborne), and 3rd Battalion, 12th Special Forces Group (Airborne) hosted me on many occasions. Thanks for the beers, the MREs, and the insights. And thanks to Bill Council, Dave Kinder, and Emmett Dover (the funniest command sergeant major in this or any other army). Also to Dennis Mack, Vahan Sipantzi, David Rodrigues, and Don Green, who each made major contributions. But the book wouldn't have happened at all were it not for Gerry Schumacher, who put more time and thought into it than anyone.

In a way, I wish they all could have their names on the title page of the book, but then somebody always has to be the commander; how else do they know whom to crucify? And, in the case of this book, that's me. But I know who supported the mission; thanks again to all.

Third Battalion, 12th Special Forces Group (Airborne), change-of-command ceremony formation.

Contents

Glossary

BDU Battle dress uniform, the camouflage uniform that is currently the approved work uniform.

Battalion Three operational companies plus supporting units providing combat intelligence, communications, transportation, and administration. About 300 people.

Briefback A sales presentation by a team after preparation for a mission. A highly detailed discussion of the intended mission.

Company In SF, a typical company consists of five or six A detachments and a headquarters group to provide administrative support. About 80 to 100 people.

Claymore A type of antipersonnel mine used in ambushes and defensive positions. It is about the size of a hardback book and uses a charge of C4 to propel several hundred steel pellets in a wide swath of death and destruction. A favorite trick of the VC was to slither up to a perimeter, turn around the Claymores, then slither back and attack. When the defenders punched the "clacker" they were thoroughly surprised. This trick didn't work with the SF teams, though. They rigged the Claymores to fire across the front of their positions; when those got turned around, it was just a waste of good explosives.

CS Tear gas. Available as powder to sprinkle on objects the enemy will come in contact with, or in grenades, which can be used in many imaginative ways.

Fast Mover Air Force jets, particularly the ones that get down on the deck to support the ground forces.

FID Foreign internal defense, one of the three basic missions of Special Forces and a peacetime variation on UW. It involves the training of friendly foreign forces in basic and advanced military skills.

FOB Forward operating base, set up by the battalion to support the units in the field.

Goatscrew Disorganized, embarrassing, graceless chaos.

Group Three battalions and a headquarters element, plus various support organizations. About a thousand people.

HE High explosive, usually TNT or "C4."

High Speed/Low Drag An expression of admiration for people who happen to be highly capable and dependable. When applied to equipment, it usually refers to something new and advanced. The M16 rifle is no longer high speed/low drag, although the little satellite radios are.

Irregular Forces Armed individuals or groups who are not members of the armed forces, police, or other internal security forces.

Klick Slang for kilometer, about 6/10ths of a mile, the standard unit of distance measurement. At the Q course, you cover a klick in five minutes or less; in the jungle, with bad guys in the neighborhood, you can spend a day moving one klick.

LBE Load-bearing equipment. Also load-carrying equipment or webbed gear. This consists of a foundation of pistol belt and suspenders and then everything you can clip, tape, or strap on, usually including magazines, canteens, strobe, and particularly a fighting knife.

LZ Landing zone, for helicopters or parachute insertion.

McGuire Rig A harness that allowed the wearer to be jerked off the ground, right up through the jungle and out of harm's way. It required the cooperation of a skilled and trained helicopter pilot, who hovered over the team's position and tossed out the ropes to which the McGuire rig was attached with a snap link. It was an exceedingly uncomfortable way of getting extracted because it meant a long ride dangling under the helicopter while it staggered back to camp. After 45 minutes everybody swore they'd never use it again—until the next time they needed to leave the party early.

MRE Meal, ready to eat. Sometimes meal, rejected by everyone. The freeze-dried meals that have replaced the older, heavier C rations.

MSS Mission support site. A safehouse or other reasonably secure location where the final administrative checks can be made before diving into the tactical area.

MTT Mobile training team. The instructors who travel to foreign lands to perform the FID mission, teaching about weapons and tactics.

ORP Objective rally point. The place the survivors gather to count noses after the assault.

Q Course Qualification course, the school for SF soldiers which begins at Camp McKall, North Carolina, and lasts about six months. Successful graduates are awarded the Special Forces tab.

RON Remain overnight position. The place you stop and hide while deep in enemy territory.

Safe Bar A special and semisacred institution with several functions, one of which is the transmission and receipt of information from indigenous personnel.

Safehouse A certified refuge from the forces of evil. During clandestine and covert operations, contacts must be made with the indigenous folk. The safehouse is a place where it happens, a little island of security in an ocean of enemy.

STABO A system like the McGuire rig which permits the victim to be plucked from the surface of the earth by a helicopter and carried back to the nest.

Sterile Devoid of identifying information, particularly things like unit patches and SF tabs.

Team A common expression for an "A" detachment of about 12 soldiers.

UW Unconventional warfare. The Department of Defense definition: "Military and paramilitary operations in enemy-held or -controlled territory." It includes guerrilla warfare, escape and evasion, subversion, sabotage, and other operations of a low visibility, covert, or clandestine nature. The operations may be prosecuted by predominantly indigenous personnel, usually supported and directed by an external source, during all conditions of war and peace.

WP White phosphorus. An incendiary material used in grenades, among other things. Causes devastating burns.

XO Executive officer, the number two guy on a team or in a unit.

Preface

They are called the U.S. Army Special Forces, and it is fitting that a book about them be written in a special way. The forces in question are select and elite societies of people; they are unique in many respects, one of which is the need for secrecy for many of their activities.

There are few things *less* secret than a book like this, the very intention of which is to be seen by as many people as possible with an interest in the subject. Some of those readers will naturally be wartime enemies who will look at these pages for opportunities and weaknesses to be exploited when and if push comes to shove. So, the security needs of the subject conflict with the purpose of publishing a book about them. That is the unconventional problem of this book.

This book was opposed by many members of the A teams—people with clandestine assignments. These people know that they are targets for assassination, that the success of their military missions requires a skillful use of the quiet arts of warfare, the first of which is silence. It properly concerns them to think that their identities and tricks of the trade will be neatly revealed to people who may one day be their enemies.

Special Forces soldiers have been the subject of books, films, magazine articles, and fantasies. Many of these have been inaccurate, mis-

---

Previous pages: Seventh Group trainer explains fundamentals of raids to young Honduran soldiers.

---

leading, improperly revealing, and silly. *Time* magazine, for example, published a major article on special operations in which Special Forces (the so-called "Green Berets") were confused with special operations forces (which include the guys in the green beanies, Rangers, Psyops, Civil Affairs, a special aviation unit, and a few other subcultures we aren't going to talk about). It might be just amusing if larger issues were not at stake. One of those issues is the life expectancy of the subjects of the article, both as individual people and as a society within the military. Another is funding, direction, and support for the units. People who design budgets and provide oversight rely to some extent on the information they get from books and magazines, and that information influences funding. It is tough to undo inaccuracies in a publication like *Time*. Or, for that matter, in a book like this one. You would think that any author who maligned a group with the reputation of the fabled Green Berets would be setting himself up to win this year's Bullet Surprise for Literature. But the men of the Special Forces are really pretty tolerant; like the rest of the military, they are used to having their missions and their personalities distorted.

But there is more to the story than that, and larger concerns. This is an important time for the special operations community, of which Special Forces is a part. The support and funding for the Rangers, SEALs, Special Forces, and the rest of the unconventional warfare organizations are suddenly on the rise. There is a lot of pressure for change and growth, which can be healthy or damaging. There has been a lot of pressure on SF to perform missions that are different from its charter, partly from a

misunderstanding of what that charter is. Some within the community think that a careful contemporary portrait can help produce more light than heat on the topic. A contemporary study like this might help explain the Forces mandate, a terrific concept that has suffered grievously in the realization. According to official records, not once in the thirty-five years of its history has the SF done what it was founded to do—perform unconventional warfare missions in denied areas.

The organization was designed and built on a foundation constructed during the 1940s, both in Europe and in the Philippines. When the Axis forces overran the poorly prepared Allies, small pockets of resistance were left within the territory controlled by the enemy. These pockets were exploited by the British Special Operations Executive and our Office of Strategic Services. They, in their small but numerous attacks, wrote the definition of unconventional warfare that we use today. Genuine UW involves operations that are (1) long term, (2) behind the lines, and (3) dependent on close cooperation with indigenous populations. Those are the three basic criteria for the SF mandate, but they are a far cry from the concept most people in and out of the military seem to have about them.

It is curious that the subject of this book is so little understood by the general public. First,

Sgt. Don Gabe, Fort Bragg, 1952. The uniform isn't—he's wearing Levi's, a field jacket, and a green beret, which was purchased at a women's clothing store and decorated with an Airborne cap patch.

This is what Green Berets actually wear in the field—the floppy, or jungle, hat. The green beanie is for more ''formal'' occasions or garrison situations.

their proper name, Special Forces, isn't even recognized by most people. But mention Green Berets and women hide and strong men tremble (or is it the other way around?). It's important to remember that the green beret is a hat, not a unit; it is worn by men in an organization called the Special Forces.

Most people think of these people we call Green Berets as a military version of the Hell's Angels, minus the long hair and the bikes. It's an impression built by decades of sloppy press. While a lot of SF people think that might be a good description of the Rangers, it is grossly inaccurate for these soldiers.

Despite the baby-killer reputation, the Green Berets are the most intellectual, intelligent, educated, creative, and constructive of our soldiers. They deliver babies, not kill them. They are required to speak at least one language besides English; many speak three, four, or five. More than that, they can *think* in three, four, or five *cultures*. They are builders and healers, besides being exceptionally well-trained and tested soldiers. And they are profoundly gifted and creative fighters, too, quite capable of embarrassing conventional forces far larger than their own.

But more important than that, they are teachers who can teach and lead novice warriors to defeat larger conventional forces, and that is in fact their principal skill and mission, the one Kennedy had in mind when he blessed them with his favor way back in 1961. The foundation of the organization, the fabled A team, is a little group of twelve men who are

The commo section tests the radios by calling up another company in the battalion, 500 miles away.

able to train, lead, and equip up to 1,500 apprentices—none of whom need speak English or know which end of a rifle to grab when they arrive at the team's doorstep.

The work of these men is as much political science as it is combat, and a successful wearer of the green beret is as skilled in interpersonal and cross-cultural relations as he is with firearms. It is these social and political skills that resulted in the alliance with the tribesmen in Viet Nam and the defeat of the guerrillas. But these skills are so alien to the public and the conventional Army that they remain essentially unknown. Historically, the Regular Army has never liked the special units, and this particular Special Force, with its odd headgear in particular, has fought both the Army and the Army's enemies since it was hatched officially back in the dark ages of 1952 A.D. But with the current interest in special operations, this is beginning to change and people are looking at SF in a new light.

Nowhere else in the military do noncommissioned officers deal so directly with the execution of American foreign policy. A great deal of their mission can be (and often is) political, with no shots fired. Nowhere else in the Army do you find enlisted men with advanced degrees, often in political science, or a junior officer in a position to influence the relations

A Special Forces trainer in Honduras. He's working with inexperienced troops, teaching the finer points of movement to contact, raids, and ambushes.

between the U.S. and another country. A junior officer may find himself working closely with a senior foreign officer as part of his assignment to, say, Nigeria, Indonesia, Honduras, or any of dozens of other small nations where mobile training teams (MTTs) may be invited. The relationship between two such people can influence relations between the countries in the near and distant future, for well or ill. So, the officer had better be skilled in much more than small unit tactics. He is a diplomat in green, and he had better be good.

Writing a book is an interesting process, and never more so than when the subject is a living legend—and one who wants to stay living. There are several ways to begin any book, one being a trip to the library to gather the things other people have written on the subject, which are then digested and reprocessed and rewrit-

Sergeant D'Asquith on a land navigation exercise at 12th Group's excellent Mountain Warfare Center. The patrol cap is proper attire for this training.

ten in a new and different form. Another is to visit the subject of the book and become part of the organization, and that's the way we do them. All of the books in the Presidio Press POWER series are based on direct, long-term, personal involvement with the subject, often over the course of years. We develop a relationship with a community within the military and get to know the character of the people and their missions and resources. We spend a lot of time following them around the skies or the seas or the backwoods of lovely Fort Bragg. We get to know them as individuals and communities, and they get to know us. The result is a different kind of portrait.

Usually, the object of our desires is flattered at the attention, and people compete for the chance to be photographed or interrogated. The American military is incredibly open and honest about its virtues and its vices, to anyone with the interest. But not so with Special Forces.

When we first started thinking about doing this book, I called a local battalion headquarters and made a preliminary inquiry. "If you show up around here with a camera," the major on the other end of the line said, "all you're going to see is a bunch of guys with paper bags over their heads." I got the idea that this was less an invitation than a warning. Nevertheless, I thought the project had merit and I called the battalion commander and the public affairs officer for the local Army area.

The commander is one of those people who elected to remain within the SF community because he loves it, and he's got a lot of company in that attitude. He also has a lot of responsibility, to the troops and to the society of the Force. Part of his responsibility is to keep his people as safe as possible while they accomplish their military mission. Another part involves the large political problem of letting other people know his unit's strengths and weaknesses, to insure that his battalion is used properly. A good book could help accomplish that latter mission, and he carefully negotiated with me to reach a mutual understanding about what this book would and would not do.

We decided to do it in a special way. This book is a collaboration with the official Special Forces community, as well as with many individuals who wear or have worn the illustrious green beret. I asked them what people should know about them, and listened carefully. I also asked them what we should not say, and learned that there were actually few problem areas. This manuscript has been carefully reviewed by a variety of SF and Department of Defense folk to make sure that nobody gets hurt.

Photographs of Special Forces soldiers, however, presented a major problem. Many of these people have assignments that might require their participation in clandestine operations, and their photographs in this book would compromise their missions and a lot of training and effort would be destroyed. With that problem in mind, we decided to generally avoid recognizable faces unless the person had no possibility of clandestine missions in the future. So we made the pictures in a more formal way than in the other POWER books, using a variety of techniques to hide identities.

But even with the help and collaboration of many of these people, there are still a lot of men within the community who are fundamentally opposed to any more books or articles that deal with the way SF does business. I have been told—more than once—that this is the first and *last* book like this that will get the cooperation of the SF troops. Perhaps one will be enough. Even so, there are troops who refused to cooperate at all. One refused to be photographed *from the back* while walking up a trail. Another, when he discovered what I was doing, started to draw his knife—in a playful rather than serious way. But the most amusing reaction came when a friend was showing me around the company he commanded; one of the troops inquired of the major who I was. "He's an author, and he's doing a book about us," the major answered. With a look of wide-eyed mock horror and a loud scream, the young staff sergeant bolted for the door and safety. I guess dealing with journalists isn't part of the instruction at the Q course. Other people said politely but firmly that they were not comfortable with the concept or the assurances, and I can't say that I blame them. They, after all, are in the running for the Bullet Surprise for International Relations.

So the support for this little volume was cautious and sometimes people were suspicious. As my friend and mentor, the battalion commander, has said more than once, with a laugh: "Hans, I *wonder* about you; this book project could be the perfect cover for somebody trying to penetrate our organization!" And, of course, he's right. In a sense, an author is a spy, but in this case, one with friendly and supportive intentions: I was working for the American reading public.

Although this is primarily a contemporary portrait, I've included a brief look at the history of unconventional warfare and the evolution of Special Forces. It is an interesting history and one that I was privileged and pleased to watch—as an outsider—early in the formative years of both Special Forces and the war in Viet Nam. I was a young helicopter door-gunner, and our company flew missions all over the Central Highlands, often into the little camps that the A teams built and operated. It was a magic time in a magic place, and I quickly became fascinated and impressed with the tribal people of the area and the amazing relationship they had with the Americans who came to live with them.

So, after all these years, it comes back again and I am honored to tell a little about those early years of conflict. It is an important story because the soldiers who wore the beret accomplished something that I think is both good and rare. It was good that they helped an oppressed group of primitive people free themselves; the freedom didn't last, but it might have. And it was rare because a group of young men from the United States Army met an extremely alien culture and became involved in positive ways. It produced a legacy very important today about how Americans can influence and become involved in conflicts. There are many ways to fight a war, and the ways of the SF are very special indeed.

First Sgt. Russ Mann has a reputation as a combat medic that goes back to the seige of Khe Sahn in 1968. Now a reservist, he is a hospital nurse in civilian life.

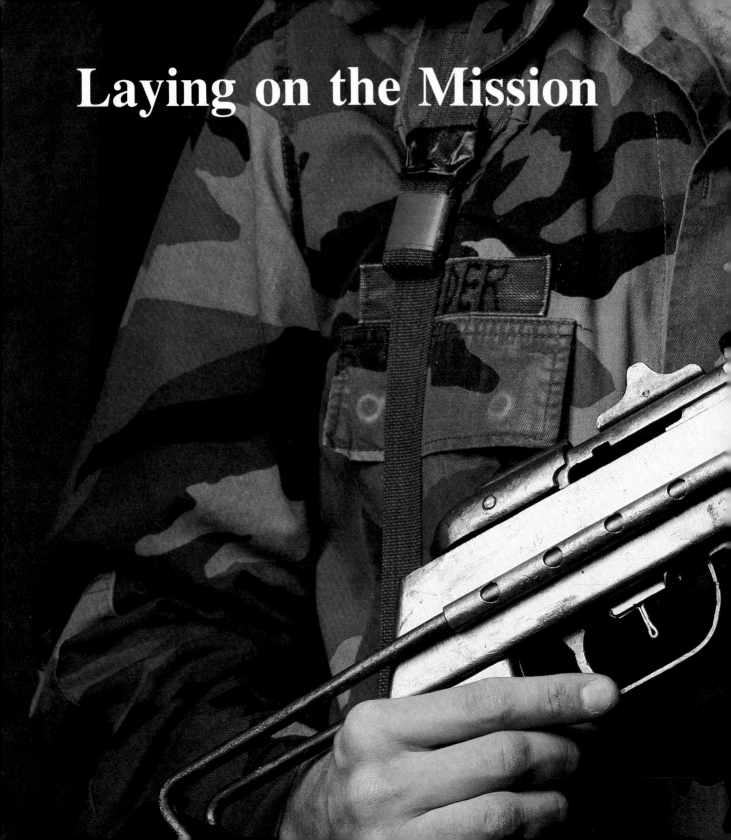

Laying on the Mission

It was long ago and far away, in a complicated place and a complicated time. The time was 1962. The place was Viet Nam.

The Central Highlands of Viet Nam were still, in 1962, a beautiful forested range of mountains, covered with tropical jungle. In the cracks and crevices of this terrain flowed rivers that drained the jungle. Here and there, where the land was level, people lived and farmed.

Although these people live in the country we call Viet Nam, you should not call them Vietnamese; they would intensely resent it, and so would the Vietnamese, because they hate each other. The mountain people are from an entirely different ethnic and social stock from the lowlanders. They are Malayo-Polynesian rather than Chinese. The words *viet nam* roughly mean "moving southward," and that is what the Vietnamese did many hundreds of years ago, displacing the original residents into the mountains. The Vietnamese word for these tribesmen is *moi*, and it means "savage," and is an insult.

The French, when they colonized Southeast Asia, called these tribal people *montagnards*, or mountaineers. About twelve major tribes—Rhade, Jarai, Sedang, Stieng, Bru, Mnong, and others—occupy the central part of the country from Dalat up to the border in towns and villages with musical names: Boun Enao, Ban Me Thout, Boun Mi Ga, Bon Sar Pa, Cheo Reo, and Plei Mrong.

In 1962 they were essentially Bronze Age people—subsistence hunters, gatherers, and farmers using slash and burn methods. They lived in small villages of communal longhouses raised above the ground, below which their livestock wandered. The men wore loincloths and the women wore skirts of carefully woven cotton cloth. Men hunted with crossbows and spears. They grew rice where they could; there isn't much farmland. There were about a million of them. And they were fighting mad.

For a group of people who like to be left alone, the tribes were getting a lot of uninvited visitors—insurgents from the north, sneaking in the back way to participate in the "liberation" of the south. They demanded support from the "primitive savages" who occupied this strategic area, forcing the moi to work for them and to contribute food.

Viet Nam Central Highlands, 1968. A successful effort in an unsuccessful war: the tribespeople, wary at first, came to trust the Special Forces soldiers.

Previous pages: Submachine gun from 12th Group's excellent collection is typical of guerrilla-quality weapons captured from the Soviets and Chinese.

14

There was no way for people with crossbows and spears to effectively resist people with firearms, so the insurgents took the rice and the tribal people went hungry. As far as the tribes were concerned, the Vietnamese from the south were not much better than or different from those from the north. For centuries, they had been insulted and displaced and persecuted. Even with a war underway, the government of the south forbade them from military service, representation in the government, or real participation in the society.

Into this equation came a few Americans: giants, aliens from another world. They listened as the tribal leaders described the problems of the highlands and asked for help. The Americans made the leaders an offer: to help the tribes protect themselves, with weapons and with training to use the weapons. The leaders accepted.

All through the mountains, dusty little muscular men with bare feet and big grins and a sense of determination started showing up in small fortified villages, lining up at the gates to join the project. They received old rifles and submachine guns and started learning which end to point at the enemy. They learned how to march, how to patrol, how to set ambushes. They were excellent students.

And slowly, they began to take back the night. In a thousand brittle engagements, the tribesmen regained control of their mountains. These Americans did more than just unload a bunch of antique firearms on the tribesmen, they came to stay and to lead and live with the people in the villages. They patrolled with them, lived with them, died with them. They learned to speak Jarai and Rhade and all the

One American, two Rhades pause in the jungle. Small patrols in the mountains beat the Viet Cong at their own game.

other languages. They were initiated into the tribal brotherhood, formally and informally. In the highlands in the '60s you could see American soldiers with half a dozen tribal bracelets on a wrist, each signifying a personal alliance and commitment to a tribe. There were many thousands of Americans in Viet Nam over the years, but the only ones the tribes accepted were the ones who wore the beret. It was an affection and loyalty that went both ways.

The story of the war in Viet Nam is loaded with untold stories of victories against the enemy, but perhaps the biggest victory was the one the tribesmen fought and won against the Viet Cong, beginning in 1962 and ending with Tet in 1968. It wasn't won by large battles between major forces, but by small encounters,

16

a patrol against a patrol. A gradual pressure on the insurgents. The hunters became the hunted, and gradually, over the years, were eliminated as a fighting force. They were replaced by the North Vietnamese regular army, all pretense of a civil war evaporated, and the fighting continued in another act of the same play.

The relationship of the United States Army Special Forces with those tribal people has become both history and heritage. The Green Berets were pulled out of the highlands in the early seventies, ordered out of the villages and back to the United States.

"They asked me: 'Will you come back?'" a command sergeant major told me of his last day there. "'Sure,' we told them, 'we'll be back!' It was the saddest day of my life." The wearing of the tribal bracelets is prohibited by Army regulations now. The young soldiers are twenty years and more older now, retired or retiring. But there are still a few who remember. I met one not long ago, a lieutenant colonel, now a Ranger battalion commander. His bracelet was worn and polished by time, like an old wedding ring that a widower might wear. Despite the regulations, he still wore it with his duty uniform.

The story of the relationship between the tribes and the United States Army Special Forces is important because there are several fundamental issues involved in what happened back then. It is instructive today both to understand who the men of the Special Forces actually are

Souvenirs from the Special Forces' time in Viet Nam: tribal cloth and bracelets from the Rhade near Ban Me Thout.

as well as to understand how they should be used—and not used—in the future.

The conventional Army looks at wars in terms of terrain, of enemy forces, of fire and maneuver—the doctrine of the AirLand Battle. Special Forces looks at the issues *behind* the conflict, at the politics and problems that lead to war. The conventional Army attains its objectives by death and destruction. Special Forces soldiers are adept warriors when appropriate, but they are also builders and healers; their most effective weapons are sometimes compassion and concern. No conventional soldier needed to learn to speak the Rhade or Jarai language. No conventional soldier lived for months in some remote collection of longhouses and became a member of the tribe. And no tribesman developed bonds of affection and loyalty toward a Marine or a common ground pounder.

"We are the last vestige of Kennedy-era liberal politics," one battalion XO told me. "We're really a military version of the Peace Corps. We are social workers with rifles." And he's right, because Jack Kennedy is the patron saint of the Special Forces. The organization predated the Kennedy administration by about ten years, but was tiny and unpopular until Kennedy became interested in it. He had a vision of world affairs and the proper place for Americans in them. Kennedy was the man who built an unconventional warfare capability, over the loud objections of the regular army. It was Kennedy who, over the (figuratively) dead bodies of a large number of general officers, authorized the wearing of the green beret. It was Kennedy and the men who built this force who saw warfare in a different light. They looked at the foundations of conflict, rather than the more violent surface. They concluded that nuclear war was more easily avoided than low-intensity conflicts, but that both could kill you 100 percent dead. And, although we as a nation worked hard to avoid nuclear war, we were doing nothing at the time to prevent casualties from the local "low-intensity" conflicts.

Since the early 1960s, when the organization was suddenly forced to expand and take on a wider role than its founders intended, Special Forces has been romanticized, trivialized, and distorted by the popular media. The result is that everybody seems to have an idea of the structure and missions of the organization popularly called the Green Berets, but very few indeed have any concept of real-world men and real-world missions. Rambo is not and never has been in an SF unit. He isn't smart enough.

SF is an exceedingly valuable asset for the American people and military, but it must be better understood if this resource is to be used effectively and efficiently, particularly in this time of transition. There are three unique and rather unknown qualities to this organization:

- It is, within the Army, a group of men at the tactical level who are taught to look at conflict in a radically different manner, in subtle political and social ways, at the *reasons behind* conflict, rather than the popular and sensational reasons found on television or in newspapers. Effective conflict resolution is a complicated business.
- These men can go to the virtual ends of the earth and develop a deep and effective relationship with the most alien of cultures, quickly developing bonds of trust and loyalty

that no other governmental organization can do.
- This very small number of men can have a decisive influence on conflict, far out of proportion to their actual numbers. (There were never more than a few thousand SF soldiers in Viet Nam, but they made a huge impact on the fighting.)

When the United States became involved in the conflicts of Southeast Asia, the intention was to help the people of South Viet Nam defend themselves and to build societies that were guerrilla-proof. It was a successful effort in the highlands and a failure elsewhere. The tribes and SF were both betrayed, and SF hasn't forgotten. Special Forces do not win wars by themselves. They are a part of the AirLand Battle and part of the Army, not an army by itself.

During the evolution of the war, SF was called on to perform many other missions, including strategic reconnaissance and strike missions, that were not part of their original mandate. They were given the missions because they were such skillful soldiers, but in a way, it was a perversion of their training and philosophy; their unique ability to deal with conflict in both military and political ways has been and still is something that makes them separate and distinct, alien and aloof, from the rest of the armed forces. It makes them difficult to understand and difficult to use well. They are, after all, Special Forces. So perhaps it is time to reevaluate their role and determine where that role properly fits in the larger spectrum of military operations, both conventional and otherwise.

Team portrait, Central Highlands about 1968. Three Americans, eight 'Yards—"a military version of the Peace Corps."

Command and Control:

The SF Mission Today

It is curious that so much attention is paid to so few people. No more than five thousand men are currently authorized to wear the beret and tab and serve in one of the eight SF groups—the approximate equivalent of a brigade of conventional forces. These are the only "real" Green Berets in the contemporary army. Special Forces units do contain other support personnel, but these people can't deploy overseas and they can't be part of a team.

Usually, when military organizations are analyzed, they are evaluated from the top down. With Special Forces, with its highly self-reliant and independent tradition, it might be better to look at things from the ground up.

The whole concept is based on a tiny foundation, the A team (or, more properly, the A *detachment*). This team is composed of about twelve carefully trained and selected soldiers. Getting into SF is much easier than getting onto one of these teams. The team is commanded by a captain; the executive officer is now a warrant officer who has been promoted from the ranks. There are a team sergeant, two weapons NCOs, two medics, two communications sergeants, two engineers, and an intel NCO on a typical team. But the numbers and structure are not carved in stone; teams can be bigger or smaller, with all sorts of permutations to the cast and crew.

The teams are part of companies, three of which combine with a headquarters unit to form a battalion, which supports and directs the teams in training and in the field. The battalion keeps the teams alive—in every respect. They provide all the supplies, the administration, and the communications. The battalion sets up the forward operating base that is the foundation of a team's efforts out in the bush.

Each battalion is an element of a group. As of this writing, there are eight groups: the 1st, 5th, 7th, and 10th are active duty; the 11th and 12th are part of the U.S. Army Reserve, and the 19th and 20th are National Guard. Each group has a headquarters company and three SF battalions, plus a service company, a signal company, and a combat intelligence company. The SF battalions have a headquarters detachment and three operational companies. Each company has a headquarters and five or six operational detachments. For operational purposes, the battalion HQ becomes what is called a C detachment; the company HQ becomes a B detachment, and the operational teams become A detachments. So each group has three C detachments, nine B detachments, and forty-five to fifty-four A detachments.

The groups and the battalions are specialists in the geographical areas in which they are supposed to operate. A group might be tasked with preparation for work in parts of Asia, for example, or Eastern Europe, or Central America, but not two of these or all three. There is a great deal of language, culture, and area study involved with an assignment to any group. Nobody wants to spend five years learning Mandarin Chinese and then get assigned to a team that is supposed to jump into Romania, for example. Not that it doesn't happen!

At this point it would be natural to ask just

Previous pages: First Sgt. Russ Mann and commanding officer Lt. Col. Gerald Schumacher outside their battalion headquarters.

22

what sort of missions SF is tasked to perform. But when you start asking questions like that around the units, you are likely to get either (1) a silent, blank look, (2) an evasive answer, or (3) "we can tell you but then we'll have to kill you." However, you've already paid for this book, so it's probably okay to tell you what they are. But this is real basic information about how SF works, so keep it confidential, okay?

UW: The first is the classic one, unconventional warfare, or simply UW. This is the stay-behind, or go-behind-the-lines job, based on the work of the OSS in France. It involves becoming part of another culture for long periods (perhaps years), organizing an effective resistance effort (perhaps without any help), and engaging the enemy in some productive way. This is what the Jedburgh teams did in France in 1944, and this is close to what the teams in the highlands of Viet Nam did in the early 1960s. It involves organizing, equipping, training, and leading people who want to resist the enemy from within occupied territory. It requires a population who wants to resist and is willing to learn the skills and accept the special hazards of a guerrilla. It is a demanding mission, requiring the special skills of interpersonal, intercultural relations; language skills; and leadership—far from friends and relations. This is the mission Colonel Bank and the other parents of SF had in mind when they conceived the force in the '50s. The expected battlefield was Germany and France.

Although this is the fundamental mission, SF has never actually performed it since the unit was hatched in 1952. They came close in Laos and Viet Nam a few times, but the behind-the-lines concept hasn't really been tried since about 1944 in Europe.

Unconventional warfare for the Army means: guerrilla warfare, evasion and escape missions, and subversion and sabotage.

Guerrilla warfare is usually thought of as operations within enemy-held territory, conducted mostly by the people who normally live there. It is supposed to help conventional forces (which are usually much stronger and likely to be decisive). Guerrilla operations are swift, brief, violent offensive actions conducted with elusiveness, mobility, and surprise. They depend on military, political, and legal considerations; the local "indigenous" population must provide support, but they also usually get external support as well.

UW (and other operations) can be overt, covert, or clandestine. In an *overt* operation, everybody can tell who did what to whom. Overt operations are not a major part of the SF bag of tricks. *Covert* operations are a little more fun: they don't try to hide the operation itself, but to conceal the identity of the sponsor. Then there are *clandestine* operations, which attempt to hide both the operation and the sponsor, as complete an attempt at secrecy as possible.

All of these themes and variations are supposed to support the AirLand Battle, either for the "unified command" or the conventional combat forces.

The unified command missions are strategic. They are interdiction missions, which ruin the enemy's day by destroying his communications or his industry, or by taking key terrain away from him. Then there is the Psyops mission, for

"Buenos dias, y'all. Now listen up!" Students in a class on "Military Operations in Urban Terrain" listen to trainers from 7th Group.

psychological operations, a way of influencing the indigenous population in enemy-held territory. When guerrilla forces are active and effective against a conventional force, the resistance movement tends to be supported. And there is also what is called an Intelligence mission, which sounds a lot like strat recon. UW forces can collect order-of-battle data, identify targets, do post-strike assessments, support specific air/ground/naval operations, and identify enemy collaborators.

Guerrillas can help the tactical commander, too. They are usually on the battlefield long before the conventional forces show up, and can be invaluable. They help the conventional forces see the battlefield, through their superior ability to conduct recon and surveillance missions. They help fight, directly and indirectly

24

supporting the conventional force. But they really shine at helping with the special problems of the local area. They know how the land lies and how to filter out the friendly civilians from the hostile ones. They are good at penetrating deep into enemy territory to get special information or to mount a raid or ambush or prisoner snatch.

FID: The second mission is called foreign internal defense, or FID. The FID mission trains governments, through their soldiers, to defeat guerrillas. It seems opposite the first mission, but in many ways they are quite similar. There are currently dozens of nations around the world who have invited the United States to send mobile training teams to improve the quality of the preparation of their forces. Honduras is one of these, and the effort is an interesting one for all hands. FID missions are part of our security assistance programs, and

Skycrane helicopter inserts a 1st Group radio team during an exercise at the 12th Group Mountain Warfare Center.

Proper form for assaulting across open space: on the run!

they are designed to help friendly governments, through their regular forces, paramilitary forces, and government agencies, to counter subversion, lawlessness, and insurgency.

STRAT RECON: Strategic reconnaissance missions involve the penetration of enemy territory to gather information about who and what happens to be where. This is a kind of spy mission and it tends to be rather hairy. Strategic reconnaissance is often considered part of the strike or direct action mission.

Then there are the special operations missions, which are sometimes separated into strat recon and strike missions. These can be executed in any of three ways: by SF people, by SF people and their indigenous friends, or by the indigenous friends all by themselves, after graduation from SF-run schools.

These missions can gain intelligence, destroy strategic targets, recover prisoners, and conduct anti-terror activities.

STRIKE MISSIONS: Strike missions are currently the popular thing in the SF bag of tricks. These are really Ranger missions, and involve short, sharp assaults against all sorts of targets. The target list, however, does not include frontal assaults on a dug-in brigade. A strike mission is supposed to be used to attack strategic targets, seize key terrain (like airheads and tactical advantage points), interdict lines of communication, support deception operations, and conduct show-of-force operations. There are some differences between the ways SF and Rangers do this kind of work; Rangers tend to work in larger units, closer to friendly territory, for shorter periods. SF can penetrate deeper, stay longer, and work with alien cultures.

Within SF are two basic communities, the active duty side and the reserve and guard component, and we will spend time with each. Traditionally, the reserve/guard contingent provides the military with a low-cost resource that becomes extremely important during times of conflict. In fact, the whole notion of the American military was founded, until recently, on the concept of the citizen soldier, the militia that kept a rifle over the mantlepiece and took it down when the nation was endangered.

Since the end of World War II, we have maintained a large standing army, a professional military. This is a major shift in American public policy, and even the military hasn't quite gotten used to it yet.

Half of the SF capability is in the full-time, active duty groups, the people who spend all their working hours being soldiers. There are four groups of them, about 2,000 people. They have a particular set of virtues in mission readiness: they can deploy for long periods overseas, they have a high degree of language qualification, they get more schools and more training than the reserve/guard. The other half are the reserve and guard soldiers, who are part-time soldiers and earn their rent and groceries doing other jobs. There are four reserve groups, about 2,000 soldiers.

So those are the people and the missions, the groups, battalions and teams, the broad-brush picture—the stuff you sometimes see in news magazines. But policies and programs can look different from real life. How do these soldiers actually go about the business of preparing for unconventional war and the other duties to which they are assigned? It is a continuous process, and a little different in each group, on each team. So let's link up with a few units and deploy for a little down-and-dirty training, both foreign and domestic.

In order to read any further, you'll need an active secret security clearance, your shots have to be current, you should have your will and power of attorney up to date, and you will need to be Airborne qualified and on jump status. Been doing your running and push-ups? Got your LBE, rucksack, and weapon? Good; let's go!

WEEKEND WARRIORS

The two A teams are gathered strategically outside a horse barn, most sitting on bales of fresh hay that have been placed on the ground for seating. Up front, two bales have been stacked to make a table, which is covered with a poncho liner. On the liner are a variety of items of tack that will be discussed during the class on horses and mules, which is about to follow. Horses and mules? Not helicopters? Not Bradley armored fighting vehicles? No, horses and mules, because that's the only kind of fighting vehicle found in the parts of the world where these two teams are planning to go. Livestock can provide transport in the mission areas, and it is only smart to plan to use available resources to accomplish the mission. So here we have two teams that, on a bright Saturday morning, have come to train on a ranch owned by the family of a member of one of the teams. The classroom is quite unlike the usual Army classroom, but it is exactly the kind that the teams will use in a UW area, and for that reason it is better than the classrooms with air-conditioning and desks.

The reserve and guard components of the armed forces are an interesting society in and of themselves. The regulars call them "weekend warriors," which is a slight on the professionalism of the people who are required to put in one weekend a month and two weeks more during the year. In some cases the insult is deserved, because some conventional units are quite casual about their commitment to fighting the AirLand Battle. But there are two societies within the weekend warrior contingent who regularly embarrass the regulars.

One of these is the Air National Guard, which is made up of aged and infirm veterans of foreign wars, flying aged and infirm aircraft of the same vintage. These old men climb into their Phantoms and lumber into the sky to do mock battle with the young puppies in their new, speed-of-heat, state-of-the-art F-14s and F-15s. And, lo and behold, the old men in their antiques latch onto the six o'clock position of the kids just long enough to make sure they are well and properly waxed, hosed, and flamed. Back on the ground the old men sometimes wear T-shirts that read "AGE AND TREACHERY WILL DEFEAT YOUTH AND STRENGTH," and the kids buy the beers.

Age, in this case, really means experience, and treachery is another way of suggesting the more subtle skills of conflict resolution. The military does some very curious things in the way that it manages its people, and one of the oddest is that it discards and discourages much of its combat experience the moment the echoes of gunfire begin to die away. So the men who have best learned the survival skills, from the bunkers to the stratosphere, are not really welcome in the peacetime army, and this is especially true of officers. If they want to retain a relationship with their service, they join the reserves.

There are two reserve and two national guard SF groups, and they are quite fascinating organizations. In some fundamental ways, they are better prepared for some missions than the regular groups. They are qualified in ways that the regulars can't achieve. They train in situations forbidden to the regular army. One of the advantages the reserve/guard contingent has is continuity. The regular army, particularly the conventional part, puts its people through a turmoil of changing assignments. Although less true of soldiers in SF, it is common for someone to be assigned to a unit for no more than three years, and then it's off to someplace else to do the same sort of job with a whole new set of people. It takes time to take the measure of the soldiers on whom you must depend, and for them to do the same for you. That time doesn't usually exist in the regular army, but it does in the guard and reserves. Many teams have members who've worked together for ten years and more. They can read each other's minds, a valuable asset in moments of crisis. They have been doing the same jobs seemingly forever, and they are all adept at accomplishing their missions. While it is true that the soldiers in the active duty groups tend to be in better shape and are more proficient at foreign language skills, the reserve and guard soldiers tend to be better at working with civilians, which happens to be one of the elements of many of their missions.

For example, there are policemen in the Los Angeles Police Department who are also SF

Members of an A team learn the basics about four-footed transport—the only kind of fighting vehicle in some parts of the world.

29

It's JMPI (jumpmaster personnel inspection) time for this team before boarding the aircraft. All Green Berets are airborne qualified.

reservists with interests in Central and South America. They deal with Spanish-speaking immigrants from Central America every day and have a personal and current relationship with the people of the area. A soldier from a regular group can't develop that rapport or practice the language without being assigned to that area. Even then, he's likely to be dealing with other soldiers rather than the civilians SF intends to convert to soldiers when a real-world UW or FID job comes along.

Then there are the medical professionals. It is one thing to go through the medical specialist training in phase two of the qualification course, and quite another to work every day in a clinic or emergency room. There are many soldiers with medical assignments on teams and in support roles whose weekday jobs involve the very things they are supposed to do in war, but for which the Army can't really provide training. The reservists with medical careers and SF responsibilities are likely to be far better qualified by experience to deal with animal bites, broken bones, allergic reactions, and many forms of illness than their counterparts in the regular units.

Everybody knows everybody else, their families, personal strengths, and weaknesses. During exercises, they refine skills that are far more subtle than the ones that the people fresh from the Q course work on. And they are loaded with people who have been to the most advanced Q course available, and that is combat time. There is no near equivalent for the sort of training you get from an extended period in a kill-or-be-killed environment, and there are fewer and fewer combat veterans in any of the active components of any of the services. But they are alive and well in the reserves, and it makes for a businesslike environment—even on a bright Saturday morning on a horse ranch.

Training activities like this always begin with something called a safety briefing, a quick reminder of the various hazards in the local environment. For today's class, a junior sergeant has been delegated to perform the briefing, and he has prepared carefully for it. He begins by discussing the several poisonous plants nearby:

Getting rigged for a jump is a team event, and sometimes you have to wait for help.

30

recognition features, effects from contact, control measures, medication options, dangers, and so on. It would be a tedious lecture for a conventional unit, but for people in SF it is important, and they all listen carefully. Instead of a simple briefing, however, what evolves is a one-hour seminar on a wide range of environmental hazards, and a rather sophisticated consideration of the ways poisons and bacteria act to create trauma. Horse bites, ticks, rabies, parasites, and poisonous plants are all considered. The young NCO is frequently assisted by

The briefback: Lieutenant Colonel Schumacher listens intently as he is briefed on an operation. He will have to decide if the mission will or will not be a "go."

members of the team who chime in with specialized knowledge. Many are health care professionals in their civilian occupations; there are paramedics, physicians' assistants, nurses, pathologists, and others who deal with medical problems in the real world every day. So, when the sergeant describes a recommended medication for the team members to use in their personal aid kits, one of the two captains breaks in: "John, that's really not a good treatment. We've been getting a lot of people coming into our clinic who've tried it and are having secondary reactions, and we're having to give them steroids to control it. Topical application of antihistamines is really not a good idea." The NCO accepts this update gracefully and goes on. A dozen times the presentation becomes a forum about things like snakes, poisonous and otherwise: how dangerous are they, how and when do they attack, what is the mechanism of envenomization? How do you treat the bite? It is a fast-paced tour of emergency medicine that is pertinent to the local area, in depth and detail, with practical uses emphasized. Tea bags,

Terrain models and sand tables are used to study tactical situations during isolation and in briefbacks.

Sergeant Mack briefs the commander. (Mack, who has been in Special Forces since the late 1960s, is the source of the "war stories" later in the book.)

it turns out, are useful for treating swollen and watery eyes from poison oak or from sun blindness. Pine needles can be boiled in water to make an effective laxative. Black widow spiders have a distinctive web that is easy to recognize. The various vectors for the transmission of rabies are discussed, which leads into a discussion of the way the disease works and how it is recognized and treated. The whole business of rabies shots is explored in a few moments as the captain describes how the shots are given and what the reactions are. An older NCO wraps up the discussion of rabies: "You want to be real careful about rabies, real careful! Once the symptoms develop, it is 100 percent fatal. It is not a pleasant way to go. I had to take care of two Montagnards, an adult female and a male

33

child, during the final stages of the disease, and it was really unpleasant! Five or six of us had to have the shots afterwards because of their thrashing around. It is not a pleasant way to go!"

Then the discussion of four-footed transport, the main event of the day, begins. Another NCO takes over and begins to discuss how and why animals can be used in UW areas, how to care for them, what their needs and capabilities are. They talk first about mules, then donkeys, horses, llamas, camels, elephants, and dogs. There is no formal Army program of instruction for these people to rely on; they have invented one themselves. They consider loads, ranges, and speeds. The NCO concludes: "Of course, this class is just an introduction, and isn't going to qualify you to take off with a bunch of animals into a UW area. You're going to have to use what you can get, whatever happens to be available where you're going. The best advice and training is going to come from the indigenous personnel. They are going to be able to teach you a lot. Listen to them!"

They split up into three groups, each of which adjourns to a horse and an instructor. Two of the instructors are SF people who own horses, and the other is a local. Everybody gets to work directly with a Horse, M1-A1, Large, and are soon cleaning hooves and practicing with pack saddles and tack. It is quite basic instruction, but there are two rather interesting considerations to it: first, it is just about the only class the Army is conducting on the use of pack animals in time of war; second, the use of pack animals is prevalent in the Third World countries where the Army expects to fight.

The SF guard and reserves are a very interesting bunch of people. They have a dedication to the organization that is religious in its zeal. They forfeit a great deal of time, normalcy, and wedded bliss for their positions on teams. Their neighbors think of them as engineers, salesmen, college students and professors, policemen, vice presidents of banks, paramedics, and sheriffs.

Although they may be called weekend warriors, they actually put tremendous amounts of time into preparation of themselves and their units. The advertised "weekend a month and two weeks in the summer" might work for other units, but not guard and reserve SF. Many of them deploy on operations, training and otherwise, for long periods. The mobile training teams in Honduras are assembled from the regulars and the reserves. The reserves go for weeks and months at a time. Deployments are an accepted part of life for a regular soldier, but for the reserves, they can be a special strain.

MISSION BASICS

No matter which mission is being performed, in training or in the real world, the ritual is the same for each.

It begins at Group, home for the Special Forces Operational Base (SFOB) that gets the mission. Missions come from several sources, some of which we don't get to talk about here. These come under the general heading of the National Command Authority—the upper strata of policy and procedure within government.

Other sources are more conventional. If a

group is responsible (for example) for a geographical area in the Pacific, the mission will probably come from CINCPAC (Commander in Chief, Pacific). SF units are typically "theater" assets, under the nominal control of the theater commander. Unfortunately, one of the other sources for missions sometimes will decide to launch an operation without telling the Group's official baby-sitter, and when that happens the theater commander and/or staff tend to blow a gasket. Missions will be run, and somebody has to pay the bills!

Most of the missions are training and preparation for the next conflict. Sometimes they will be large-scale exercises with SF playing a small role. They can be training missions overseas, in quiet and friendly places like Australia or more nervous places like El Salvador. The teams can be supporting huge operations involving large conventional Army, Navy, and Air Force units who will be fighting a simulated version of the AirLand Battle, just as they expect to in real war.

But regardless of source, a mission is layed on, and is passed on to an appropriate forward operating base, which is operated by a battalion. The teams are launched and run from the FOB, which serves as an operations center. The battalion commander hangs out here to run the show, when he's not running around out in the field.

A major part of the FOB is the communica-

"Commo" is the heart of any operation. Commanders want to know what is happening while it is happening.

tions center, a vital element of the whole production. Clear, secure, timely communications are important to both ends of the chain of command: the sponsors of the show want to know what is happening while it is happening; the teams need to coordinate the support and assistance they require as the mission evolves.

There are lots of ways to chat with your friends—most of which are easily intercepted by your enemies. They use UHF, VHF, FM, and satellite transmissions. They use elaborate antennas and wire fences. There is a small, collapsible antenna for satellite communications, and when and if you can get the use of one of the channels on the satellite, you have the ability to plead with full clarity and eloquence with the people back at Bragg or wherever for more beer and grenades.

And there are all sorts of devices to encode and decode messages, to condense them for "burst" transmission, and for other ways to communicate. With the right piece of hardware, you can walk up to a pay phone in downtown Leningrad and make a quite secure call to one of your FOB friends back at the ranch. The burst transmission device allows you to record a message that would take many minutes to transmit in real time, but that can be compressed and blasted out into the ether in just a few seconds. Since you and your compadres back at the ranch know when and what frequency you will use for the message, the com-

---

Here's where the things they taught you at Q Course come in handy. Rappeling from a UH-1 helicopter with full combat equipment.

munication will get through. But since there are too many frequencies for the bad guys to monitor all the time, they have to wait until you start to transmit before they can lock on to your signal to eavesdrop. With any luck, by the time they have tuned in, you have tuned out. That's the idea of burst transmission.

The commo guys are the technical heart of the operation, and they own many of the most interesting and secret of the toys in the inventory. But they also learn early in phase two of the Q course how to use old chunks of wire to make effective antennas and how to fix radios with almost nothing. They can communicate with almost anything short of two cans and a string . . . and maybe even that, on occasion.

Sometimes the commo section would probably prefer to use two cans and a piece of string, because the Soviets and their allies have excellent intercept systems. They can, within just a few seconds and from thousands of miles away, pick up and identify a transmission, read the traffic, and tell you where the transmitter is located. The transmitter, of course, tells you where the team is . . . and if you'd like to get together for a visit, you now know where to find them. The time when that team is transmitting, kicking their message off into the ionosphere, is one of the scariest parts of an operation.

The FOB gets set up first, followed by the arrival of the B detachments and the A teams. The B detachment will serve as the local administrator, taking care of much of the supply and communication work that the A teams will need while they attend to business. The teams arrive and enter the rarified world of "isolation." The term is appropriate: until the operation is declared over, each member of the team is cut off from every aspect of normal life not related to the mission. When you step into the FOB and into isolation, you leave the normal world behind. Wives, children, friends are all separated from you by a gulf of ritual and regulation. Isolation is used by many elements of the armed forces special operations community. It is an effective way to insulate the people who are trying to accomplish the mission from the many forces that conspire against them. It can be a pain, but there are worse pains readily available in the world of clandestine operations.

In-processing takes about an hour and a half. The support team makes sure wills and powers of attorney are current and correct. Medical and

Down we go! Rappeling is a fundamental Special Forces skill.

37

personnel records are checked in detail.

As the teams complete the in-processing, they are given their target folders and mission statements; then they move to the building where they will be isolated. It is heavily guarded.

Ten A teams may go into isolation, but they will not come in contact with each other; isolation is complete. There may be ten missions—or one. The team that shows itself best able to accomplish the mission will be "good to go" and the other nine will sit tight until they get back.

For a day or so they review the data in the folders. It is homework time in a big way; the information is studied with particular enthusiasm, though, because the final examination is potentially a life-or-death test.

Then the FOB commander and his staff brief the team on the mission as they perceive it in the broadest sense. It is an overview of what needs to be done and the resources available to do it, but little if anything on how to put the resources to work. The design of the mission is the teams' job, the one they have trained to do, rehearsed and anticipated. It is a highly creative job, but they have a lot more homework to do before they even begin the design phase.

The briefing lasts for hours and covers all sorts of details related to the mission.

"You will not be receiving resupply during the mission period. . . ."

"There is a resistance movement in the area that may provide you with some support, but watch out for them because there are some hostile factions within the group who may want to kill you. . . ."

The briefing covers climate, culture, enemy and resistance elements, terrain features, logistics, religion, transportation, airfields that might be useful, and much more.

The FOB is an Army operation, but it is heavily augmented with support from the Air Force, often from the Navy, and perhaps elsewhere. There are weathermen, aircraft specialists, and the rest. The team and their commander need to know about winds and tides and runways and resistance movements. Each specialist spends an hour or two with the team, providing information that will help the team with the creative process. While the men are listening, they begin formulating their plan. It is a group effort, and the team leader is the moderator. They also prepare in other ways: they test fire their weapons, do radio checks. They may get training on a specialized aircraft, although that presents problems. While in isolation, nobody in the outside world is supposed to see them; so how do they travel out of the compound, off the base, to an airfield somewhere, without being seen? It takes a lot of planning and forethought to prevent compromise of the mission.

The FOB might not even look like an SF FOB. Operations have been run where all the berets and patches and other identifying details come off the uniforms, and the baseball caps and civilian clothes go on and everybody walks around saying "Who, me? I don't know nothing 'bout no Special Forces!" Sometimes they change into other military uniforms, and sometimes into civilian clothes. It can be amusing, because there are places (like Honduras) where all these big muscular gringos with the guns under their shirts stand out in spite of the civilian clothes.

When the staff and the commander are done

with their lectures, the team gets to interrogate them about details they want clarified. Then they are led back to their cells. For the next five or so days (a typical period that can be much longer), each of the FOB staff will go in and provide highly detailed briefings on aspects of the mission. The communications officer may say: "For the purpose of your operation, we will be giving you a new and highly secret radio that weighs half an ounce, will send burst transmission of 20,000 characters a second, and can provide clear comms with us from anywhere on the surface of the earth. Not only that, it contains a small explosive device, and you can use it as a very powerful hand grenade if absolutely essential." He and his helpers may then spend hours training members of the team to use this new radio that may be essential to the accomplishment of the mission.

The very freshest satellite photos are provided. Even while the teams are in isolation, the Air Force will run F-4 recon flights over the target and supply daily snapshots of the area. This recon function can be—and has been—a weak link in the process. In 1970 a raid was carefully designed and executed to release a large number of fliers held prisoner by the North Vietnamese at a prison called Son Tay, near downtown Hanoi. It was a perfect raid in every respect, except that there were no prisoners in the prison, the NVA having moved them some weeks before the event! Good photo recon should have shown that the place was abandoned, but there was no good photo recon. Interservice support has been and still is a problem for special ops.

Even the chaplain gets involved in the briefings, and can provide exceedingly useful information: what are the religions in the target area; who is most likely to be supportive of the U.S.; are there printing presses in the churches that could be used to produce leaflets for Psyops missions, and on and on. (And after the briefing, he says, "Bless you, my son; is there anything you want me to tell your widow?")

Another briefing may come from a very special source—a member of a resistance group within the target area who has been smuggled out and into the FOB to provide detailed and up-to-date information. This is called an asset brief. Only one member of the team will actually talk directly to the "asset," to preserve as much security for the team as possible. Even then, the person may be held in isolation for the duration of the mission.

THE BRIEFBACK

At the end of the briefing and planning period, the team will have developed its plan and polished it to a high gloss. By now each man has committed to memory hundreds or thousands of pieces of information: radio frequencies, grid coordinates, times, names of contacts, most of which will never be written down. Before the team leaves isolation, they will have "sterilized" themselves: no marked maps, uniforms bare except for the U.S. Army tape, no grid coordinates, no information about adjacent units. Everything is committed completely to memory.

The next step is a presentation that may be the essence of special operations, the briefback. For the past five or so days, the team has been creating a solution to a problem. This solution is a kind of elaborate script, which is officially called a tactical operations order. There are usually a multitude of ways you can mix and match the resources available to accomplish a mission; the creative part of special ops comes with the way your team solves the equation. Before you can go anywhere, you present your plan to the FOB commander and his staff, the very people who briefed you at the outset. They originally told you what you were supposed to accomplish and what you had to accomplish it with; now they want to see how you are going to effect the mission.

The purpose of the briefback is to convince the FOB commander that the team is capable of executing the mission and coming back alive. It is not unheard of for an FOB commander to say to the team at the conclusion of a briefback: You're a no-go. Your plans will not wash. It is devastating for a team to hear, but it happens. The commander and his staff ask lots of questions and they expect to hear accurate and detailed answers: what are the six most common diseases you will find in that area? And the commo guy (not just the medic) will have to know. The medic may be asked: what are the five alternate frequencies you're going to use for this kind of burst transmission? And the medic better know what they are. The assistant team leader will have to know the details of the work the demolitions men will do. How long is the runway? How do you know it will support the weight of the aircraft? What is the condition of that runway? What are you going to do if you

Sniper skills are part of the routine for many team members. Here a sniper and spotter in camouflage ''ghillie'' suits blend into the terrain while lining up on targets.

40

get out there and the runway has great big stakes and bulldozers on it? What's your alternate plan? Every plan has to have two, three, or four alternatives. What do you do if you lose a helicopter en route? At what point can you no longer execute that mission?

As one officer says, "At what point is my no-go really going to be? I don't want to be on the ground in the middle of an event unfolding and not have thought out this event beforehand; to be able to say to myself, well, I *knew* this was going to happen, that we were going to get into a dust storm and lose two helicopters . . . and I knew that if this happened, I was going to do such and such.

"Not every conceivable event can ever be considered. There will always be something that you couldn't have forecast properly, and then you're up to your ass in alligators, and you improvise like hell. But a briefback, in my

The briefback is the climax of the 5-day isolation process. A plan is presented—the team's solution to the problem.

"That's a good plan. You're a go!"

estimation, is the most singularly impressive representation of SF knowledge and preparation for combat that you could possibly see. Because if the FOB staff is sharp, and if the A team is sharp, you will hear question after question, and answer after answer, that reveal incredibly detailed knowledge. The team had better know; that's what the five days, and the years of training, are supposed to have accomplished.''

Briefbacks are used by SEALs, Rangers, Air Force para-rescue teams, and others, but the level of sophistication and detail is unique to SF. Everybody has to know how to do nearly everybody else's job, so that when someone is killed, the other people on the team can drive on and finish the mission. This is the essence of Special Forces.

At last, the commander looks the team leader in the eye; he has weighed the hazards and the plan, the preparation and the resources.

"Okay. I think it'll work. You're a go."

Launching the Mission:

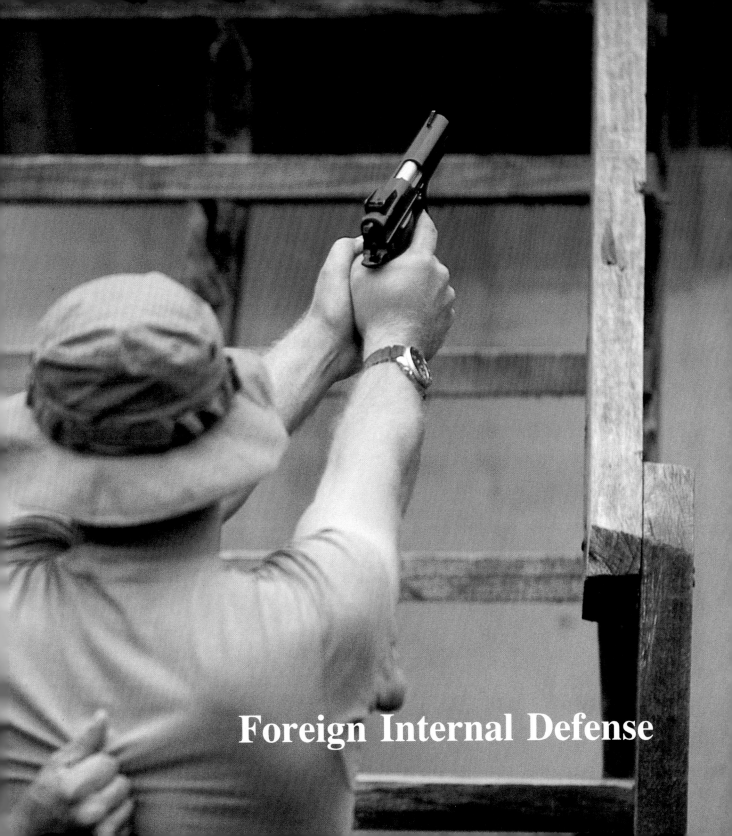

Foreign Internal Defense

There are still spent cartridge cases in the street, long after the assault. There are bullet holes in the side of the church, and all that remains of the little barracks where the government outpost used to be is the foundation. It is still painted in a camouflage pattern, but the guerrillas saw it anyway. The rest was burned.

Down the street at the corner is a little memorial, but it has nothing to do with the soldiers who were killed when the guerrillas attacked the town; this one is for a former town secretary. On another visit, they put him up against a fence post and shot him—for no special reason—as an example to the rest of the population: here's what happens when you cooperate with the official government.

It's a lovely town, halfway up the side of a momentarily quiet volcano. There are no phones in the place, and the only contact with the rest of the world is a single telegraph line, easily cut. The main highway is ten klicks down the worst road in the Western Hemisphere. It is caught in a time and culture warp, in conflict and in tranquility.

The army still patrols here, but now it is one of the companies from down by the main road; when they move through town, it is with flankers out, and they all have hunter's eyes. It is an active rather than a passive sort of defense. That means the troops don't man a little garrison in town anymore; if they are around at all, they are out hunting in the jungle. They look serious and businesslike and professional. Maybe that's why the Gs (as the guerrillas are often called) haven't been back for a year now.

Until recently, child mortality here was 80 percent. The place is loaded with parasites; malnutrition is common; the soil and terrain are good for growing coffee and nothing else. When the price of coffee is up, there is work for the men; when it is down, they don't work and their families don't eat much. In spite of it all, the people are clean and cheerful.

Throughout the rural areas of Central America, and many other places around the world as well, there are little towns like this, under stress. It is a fertile place for insurgencies to develop, and they do. Anybody can sympathize with the unrest. The guerrillas would be more successful if they were not so clumsy.

Way back in 1961 President-Elect Kennedy was looking at similar situations when he foresaw the need for a special kind of warfare. The need hasn't gone away. It is in this kind of environment where SF is most effective and where it should be most active.

There are reasons for wars, and neither side is ever all good or all bad. In Central America and elsewhere, people and their governments struggle with the problems of economics and disease. Some of these governments must deal with insurgencies as well. Their resources are severely limited, and improving their societies is extremely challenging. Their armed forces have few of the resources we take for granted. It is a complicated, difficult situation, without easy questions or answers. Should we isolate ourselves from the issues and let them resolve

Previous pages: Two trainers from 7th Group demonstrate proper form while clearing a building. The hand on the shirt keeps them in sync while they move up the steps, allowing each to watch separate areas.

themselves one way or another, or do we get involved? We have decided to get involved—in a very small way.

Many people have the idea that SF units deploy overseas *only* on missions that are violent invasions of foreign countries, sneaking in to shoot up the place. Reality is less sensational. Governments all over the world request training from SF mobile training teams, who deploy on their missions with the cooperation and support of the Department of State as well as the Department of Defense. Nigeria, Honduras, Korea, the Philippines, Thailand, Australia, El Salvador, Canada, and many others, all over the globe, ask for SF training teams to instruct on some aspect of the military profession that the host nation needs and that the teams can provide. Some of these nations are pressured by insurgencies, but many are not. When these teams are deployed, it is a mission like any other. They prepare by doing their homework. They are launched and supported by an FOB; the A teams in the field are backed up by a B detachment and its commo section. It is training in the real world, and the training goes both ways. Because of the threat level, only fifty-five trainers are currently allowed to be in El Salvador at any one time. Honduras, however, is more peaceful and a lot of training is done there, of both Hondurans and Americans.

Bullet hole in a fence post where this Central American town's mayor was assassinated by guerrillas. Real-world threats are encountered in FID training.

In Central America the training tends to cover basic information. The soldiers of many of these countries might fire only ten rounds through their rifles during all their basic training. Their countries have little money for things like ammunition, and they have few people qualified to instruct the troops. Their military tradition is different from ours: there is no professional enlisted corps. Troops are drafted, serve their two years, and leave the service, taking with them whatever experience and in-

In Third World countries where situations are ripe for armed conflict, governments sometimes ask for assistance from SF mobile training teams.

sights they acquired. They tend to be very young.

The government of Honduras has asked for MTTs to augment the training of several units of their army. Seventh Group is tasked with that geographical area of responsibility and consequently gets the nod. Elements of the

Twelfth Group are tasked to support with additional A detachments. An FID exercise is planned, organized, and launched, with the teams flying out of Fort Bragg and into the base the USAF has developed at Palmerola. It looks just like Viet Nam, but smells better. In Honduras, although the threat level is pretty low, there is still some possibility for isolated attacks on individuals and groups. So we wear civilian clothes; on the seat of the car, when we drive, is a pistol. When we go to dinner in the village, one of us will be inconspicuously armed with a .45. We don't get too comfortable, even in quiet Honduras.

The operation will be run by the B detachment from a little compound near a northern industrial city. The Hondurans have a little post there, home for an infantry battalion. In some small officers' quarters (fully equipped with cold showers) the B team and several A teams set up

A young trooper from Honduras learns the drill from 7th Group trainers. He pays close attention—he will be off on patrol by the Nicaraguan border in a few weeks.

shop. The antennas are erected, generators tested, radios switched on, and there's Fort Bragg on the line. And greetings to all our listeners in the Soviet bloc, too!!

One of the teams goes off to a village where another battalion of Hondurans has a home port. These guys are sharp, well trained, and don't need the fundamentals that other units will be teaching. These troops will be learning the subtleties of urban combat. The team sets up in a rather elegant home left by a recently departed contractor. It would be a lot nicer if the water that came out of the tap didn't look like chocolate milk!

The training routine is quite mixed. One of the teams will train soldiers fresh from basic. They look younger than they are, which is still late teens. They have very little experience with their weapons and less with the fundamental military skills of patrolling. They are about to get a short but intense course in the fine art of small unit fire and maneuver. And they'll need it: they are going off to the Nicaraguan border when they are done, and they don't use blanks down there.

Over the course of several weeks, the trainers and the trainees both learn a lot. The SF trainers practice one of their fundamental missions—instructing indigenous people to defend themselves. It puts to work the language and cultural skills in a big way.

One of the reservists, a medical specialist in his civilian career and a medical specialist in SF, has spent many months in Central America. Like others on the MTT, he's a veteran of SF combat in Viet Nam and can compare times, places, people, and events. Like the other vets, he often compares Central America and South-east Asia, and there is a lot to compare. The similarity of the terrain is amazing. But there are important differences, too.

We get a lot of good experience in a low threat environment, but it is very real world, with important strategic objectives for the other side as well as us. We get some excellent training, and so do the Hondurans. The host countries naturally have trainers, but they tend not to be as experienced as we are; we have a lot of people who are experienced in guerrilla warfare and interested in FID missions. So they get good training and get to think about things they would otherwise not consider.

It is also a morale boost for them; if we're out in the field with them, sweat with them, eat their food and drink their beer, then, by God, they appreciate what we're doing and what we're going through.

I am a dedicated anti-communist. Anything I can do to frustrate the other side, I will do. If I can help build a strong Honduran armed force, supporting a government that is—if not purely democratic—the most democratic in this century, I'll do it. I have fun working with those people; they're very receptive to what I have to offer. I can actually see concrete results, especially in the medical area. I also get some experience in medicine that I don't see every day in my clinic here in the States.

I hope and pray that, with the abundance of experience in both the active duty and reserve sides of the house, in guerrilla warfare and FID, that we aren't making a lot of the same kinds of mistakes we made in Southeast Asia. Things like halfhearted civic action, inadequate defensive positions, and inadequate support for the units that we field. As an old field soldier I feel

Before a walk-through of a raid rehearsal, Honduran students listen to a 12th Group trainer.

strongly that we shouldn't let that happen. No-body's listening; the same old conventional mindblock takes over. That base at Palmerola is another Pleiku waiting to happen.

The trainers begin to put the young troopers through the same instruction that is given in phase one of the Q course on patrolling, raids, and ambushes. There is a little difficulty at first with the language, because some of the trainers haven't become proficient yet in Spanish. But one of the troops was a law student in Los Angeles, and his English is good; he translates when the instructor gets stumped. The class-room is an open air shelter that keeps off the sun. There are benches for the students, and a small blackboard. The trainer explains the basics; first it is simple patrolling. Then they all go out and try it. At first the students bunch up, look at the trail, and make too much noise.

They don't know anything about immediate action drills, but they soon learn. They're a willing bunch, bright eyed and energetic. They begin to learn about security teams, bounding overwatch, and fire and maneuver. It is fast paced; nobody is bored or sleepy.

Left: Ready for the assault, students are positioned by the trainers. *Below:* Grenade simulators and muzzle flashes signal the beginning of the Honduran students' raid on a hilltop position.

Then they start to learn about raids and ambushes, and it gets even more interesting. First, an hour or so in the classroom, then out to rehearse the moves. The classroom itself will serve as the target. The students form up on line, just out of sight, then rush the building. One of the instructors role-plays an enemy casualty, lying face down on the dirt. The assault element runs to him; one man covers him while another turns him over to look for his pistol. The troops are learning their lessons.

Later, just at dusk, a more demanding test is

The proper way to search a body. A pistol or grenade could be hidden between body and ground.

A young Honduran trooper listens intently to his instructions before a rehearsal.

given. The students will move up on and assault a hilltop position in the nearby jungle. The defenders—the bad guys—will be the American trainers. The Hondurans are doing this for the first time, and they are working hard at doing it well. Just the same, the Americans can see the Hondurans trying to sneak up on them through the brush. Just before dark the sound of an M60 breaks the quiet of the evening, followed by the sounds of M16 blanks and grenade simulators exploding on the position. The attackers sweep rapidly through the position and take up positions on the far side, while the "dead" defenders are checked; there are weapons and grenade simulators hidden under all of them. Then they pull back and evaporate into the jungle. Not perfect, but a pretty good performance from people who've been doing this only for a week or so.

The instructors get up and dust themselves off. "Did you see the looks on their faces?" one asks. "Boy, they were really into it!"

Later on that evening the trainers head into the little village near the compound for dinner and a few Port Royal Exports in one of the two local restaurants; they trade off, to spread the business around. It is the perfect time and place for an after action review. Who really gets the better training? It's hard to say. The team members are impressed with the energy and intensity of the troops, but complain that they are so young and immature that it will take many months of training and experience before they will be very effective combatants. And by then, they will be out of the service. The lack of a professional enlisted core in these armies is a real handicap and a frustration for the teams. These lessons will have to be retaught continuously. But, on the other hand, this is exactly the kind of training the SF soldiers would do behind the lines if the balloon goes up for Round Three, so it is a wonderful opportunity for practicing a part of the UW job.

Most of the team members are veterans of many other MTT missions, and the conversation turns to a comparison of the experiences they've had over the years. Canada, for example, invited some of them to teach a short course on foreign weapons, a specialty of this particular unit. So they bundled up the AKs, the SKS carbines, the heavy and the light machine guns—foreign and domestic—and headed off to the great white north. They set up a short block of instruction as part of the Canadians' excellent Battle School, instructing on both foreign weapons and on night vision devices, neither of which the Canadians have in large quantities. Members of the Canadian battalions were rotated through, a platoon at a time. The Canadians reciprocated by running two A teams through the complete school, which features an excellent and highly challenging "live fire" exercise.

At the conclusion of almost every MTT deployment comes an absolute frenzy of horse trading, and this one is no exception. It is an event that experienced team members enjoy more than any other part of the deployment. It seems that every army comes up with some item of equipment or uniform that is excellent in some way or other, and inspires envy in the soldiers of other nations. So it is common for SF teams to board the aircraft for home in civilian clothes or the last set of BDUs, everything else having been traded or given away. In return, they have obtained excellent sleeping bags, boots, and sweaters.

Forty-five days after they arrive, the teams pack their gear and prepare to go home. Back at the air base at Palmerola, a C141 waits for them. Another set of teams is on the way to take over. The job isn't glamorous, but it is one of the missions of the Green Berets.

"Okay, get out there and move!" It's a full daylight rehearsal of a raid.

Actions at the Objective:

Strike Missions

So, you want to go along on a real SF mission, to see how it actually works? Okay, no problem!

Our detachment, team A814, receives the mission in a briefing from the FOB commander and staff, in isolation. We've been given the mission of assaulting a nuclear weapons storage area (NWSA) and capturing or destroying a particular nuclear weapon in a specific bunker on the heavily defended compound.

During the briefing we are shown photographs and maps of the target. Somebody has been able to penetrate the defenses to get pictures of the details of the bunker doors, right down to the way the hinges and locks are made. We also receive detailed information about the terrain, weather, escape and evasion routes, and more. We get a full briefing on what is known about the weapon, and what we are supposed to do with it when we get it.

We are briefed on the defenders: about a company of them, all professional security specialists, equipped with two armored cars and a liberal supply of automatic weapons. There are several buildings on the compound, one of which houses the vehicles and the reaction force. The road will probably be blocked. The compound is ringed with two high chain-link fences, topped with razor wire; there are two guard towers; sensors in the ground to detect movement; and a double gate, operated from inside a guard bunker with bulletproof glass. The terrain surrounding the NWSA is wide

The bunker wherein dwells a notional nuclear device, the objective of an SF training assault.

open, without a tree or other cover for many hundreds of meters. And—won't this be fun—the defenders are expecting us.

So, we'll be outnumbered ten to one by an enemy who is supposed to be a professional at defeating people like us; who has all sorts of tactical and terrain advantages; and who knows, almost to the minute, when we will arrive on his doorstep. Still want to go?

On the other hand, we do have some advantages. We can maneuver against a force that is tied down to its compound. We can accomplish our mission in all sorts of ways, many of which will be unexpected. We can cheat like crazy. We're going to play the role of Soviet special operations forces against an American unit. We are the bad guys.

Special Forces units are often tasked with training other American forces, particularly tactical units of the Army, Air Force, and Marines. The Special Forces soldiers know how to play the role of guerrilla fighters, and have direct action missions against much larger forces. Although raids and ambushes by the sort of irregular and unconventional little forces that SF teams represent are an expected part of war, they still frequently drive the conventional force commanders totally nuts.

Many of the war stories that circulate in SF units are based on peacetime events, and the "enemy" is often an Army battalion, brigade, or division. These "enemy" units have ways of preparing for combat that are carefully orches-

trated and scripted. They get into patterns of behavior that help them do well on the AR-TEPs, but that are hazardous to their health in conflict. These units are used to fighting against similar-sized conventional units that play by the same rules. The evolutions are roughly predictable and seldom very dramatic. But not when the SF units get to play. For example:

- A fire truck with lights and siren going full blast screams up to the gate of a compound during an exercise and it is quickly admitted by the heavily armed but helpful guards. Once inside, the firefighters pull M16s from under the hoses and capture the position from the startled—and then furious—defenders.
- Two bow hunters, with long hair and beards, one with an eye injury, seek help from soldiers in the field and are directed to the field hospital colocated with the division tactical operations center (TOC). They are checked by the suspicious sentries, who have been warned about the games SF can play and who know that guerrillas are part of the exercise; but both hunters have valid bow-hunting licenses and seem legitimate, and the eye injury is pretty gross. So the two civilians are admitted and pointed toward the clinic to have the eye attended to. Once safely away from the guards, the hunters change course for the division TOC. The "injury," the result of skillfully applied make-up, is quickly discarded. From the quivers come blocks of simulated explosives, which are expertly placed and set. The hunters walk away. The exercise referees declare the TOC destroyed, and the party is over for the commander and his staff.

The doors to the bunker must be blown open. The team has to calculate the amount and type of explosives required, and place them correctly before the referees will allow them inside.

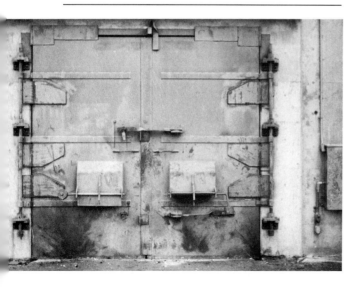

The process of preparing for special combat is different. In a conventional unit, the individual soldiers receive their warning and operations orders, then move out in fire teams, squads, platoons, and company formations. The individual troop has very little involvement in the planning and design of the operation. But in an SF operation, preparation and design of the mission is a whole team activity, and the individuals all conspire to come up with the most creative solution to the problem they've been given. It's their job, unlike the conventional units, to design the way the mission is accomplished.

In our case, we've been told that we have to get control of a nuclear device that is stored in a compound, guarded by a large and professional force. But (and this is important) we haven't been told how to get in, or out, or how to deal with the opposition. If we think we can tunnel underground and into the bunker—and can prove we can do it—that will be our plan.

We have been challenged to be creative in an art form where success and failure are life-and-death issues. In our particular training exercise, no one will actually be killed, but many of the players in the game will know that, in a real encounter, they would have been killed or wounded. Training exercises are far removed from the tensions of real combat, but there are passions involved just the same. Professional pride is a strong motivator. Everybody wants to

Ready for the assault. This M60 machine-gun is decorated with Miles transmitter and a belt of blank cartridges.

do well, to embarrass the other team. The referees carefully tell the players that there are no winners or losers in these encounters, that everybody is a winner because everybody learns lessons that they can apply in real combat. That still doesn't prevent both sides from trying to totally wax the opposition.

Although nothing in peacetime training comes close to the thrill of the snap, crackle, and pop of little chunks of metal zipping past your ear, the Army is using a laser system called MILES to help people in these war games know when they are hitting and being hit. These exercises are taken seriously by the players, because they are as close to real combat as the units are permitted to get (as of this writing). The MILES system works well for scoring

A member of the SF team, an ROTC student, waits for the play to begin. On his hat he wears a MILES receiver; the transmitter is on his rifle.

61

An artillery simulator is a lot like a grenade, but with cardboard shrapnel. It is smart to handle them with respect.

the accuracy of direct fire weapons like rifles and machine guns, but doesn't work for indirect fire weapons, like mortars; it isn't set up to work with LAWs or recoilless rifles either, so its use on this exercise will be only partially effective.

This kind of training is a good workout for both sides. Our team is going to practice "actions at the objective," the way the team works while it is actually assaulting a position. We don't get to do this a lot, and it is fun. It is practice for the direct action or strike mission rather than the UW role, and some of the people on the team really prefer it. Ranger work!

The defenders, who spend most of their professional lives standing by a gate, asking to see people's ID cards, bored right out of their minds, will be entertained for thirty-six hours or so with some intense and unexpected action. They will come away from the exercise just a little better prepared—as individuals and as a unit—to deal with several variations on the theme of small unit assaults on the compounds they guard. They will be exposed to threats that they have never considered, and after being killed a time or two, they will remember them well and consider them carefully, even when they are checking ID cards at the gate.

This operation, like all others, is referred to by a code name rather than a clear description; it is Operation NINJA. This helps to insulate the operation from the hazards of compromise. In military operations generally, and in special ops in particular, surprise is much of the battle. Consequently, all the individuals, the units, the locations of the target, and all the other support sites are referred to by code names. These names are maddeningly similar, and for this operation they happen to include NAPPY, NANNY, NORSE, NEEDY, NOBLE, and about twenty others. You'll have to memorize them all and what each represents. In addition, each team member must remember that SUNRISE means the mission is a go; SUNSET means the mission aborts; HIGH NOON means the teams are in position; RAINING means the mission has been compromised. Try not to get them confused.

This preparation gets complex when the various permutations are considered and planned for. SUNRISE is supposed to be at 1000, but it can go early, or late. No matter what time it is scheduled to go, the attack will be initiated with one of several possible signals.

The code name for initiating the attack will be SUN BURST, and it can be triggered by a white flare or white smoke; another signal could be when the assault team fires on the compound or gets through the gate.

Several days before the operation, the team leader does his final recon of the target. He has been studying it for weeks now and has developed an imaginative plan to get past the double gate, past the armored cars, past the defenders, and into the bunker. He is going to cheat.

Well, okay, it isn't really cheating, but the plan does include some elements that the defenders are not used to facing in exercises.

One is an ambulance, and it will be used to transport the assault team to the gate and perhaps to bring out the bomb.

Another is a pretty blond young lady in an

63

Air Force uniform, who will play the role of a medical specialist.

And finally, we will be using nerve gas in large quantities. *Of course* it's illegal! That's what helps make it effective! We are, after all, Soviet "Spetnaz," and we don't have to play fair.

An essential element of an operation like this is the location and security of support sites. We will have to travel several hundred miles to the area of the compound. On the way, we will stop and make preliminary preparations. Weapons will be inspected, ammunition inventoried (but not distributed), MREs handed out, final plans made. All this happens at the mission support site (MSS). From there, we will move out to a secure location very near the target, the objective rally point (ORP), where we will make our final preparations.

The tactical plan is pretty amazing. For starters, this compound is wide open for a HALO assault, and one is planned. HALO stands for high altitude (exit from aircraft), low opening (of parachute). It is one of the several excellent ways available to the special ops community to insert people into places where they are not welcome. To make a HALO jump, you get the Air Force to fly you over the general target area at some extreme and essentially invisible altitude—25,000 feet will work. Then you and all your gear jump from the plane and free fall like a sky diver while guiding yourself to the target

and then opening your black canopy at an absolute minimum altitude above the ground. It works best at night, when it is an extremely sneaky way to drop in for a visit. And, on this operation, it would just about guarantee that some of us will make it at least to the top of the bunker.

The Air Force, however, decides it doesn't have a functional airframe to support the mission, so we fall back to plan B.

We will be limited to a ground assault. The assault will be conducted by three groups: a security element, a surveillance element, and an assault element. Although the attack will last only a few minutes, the preparations develop over days in steadily increasing intensity. The mission planning begins weeks before the

An Air Force "traitor," recruited to help with the strike mission, is briefed by one of the SF team in his UW uniform.

Left: The team leader (*foreground*) explains the plan to the Air Force controller, part of the host team.

actual assault; in addition to all the information the FOB staff provides, the team leader elects to infiltrate himself into the area to recon the situation and see what variations are possible to help in the assault.

On one of these recons, he meets a young Air Force enlisted woman and carefully recruits her to help with the attack. She is invited to play the role of a traitor, and she cheerfully accepts.

Thirty hours before the assault is scheduled to go, the team draws its weapons and MILES gear, dumps rucksacks and LBE into vehicles, and mounts up. The mission support site, where the final preparations will be made, is two hours away. The objective is another hundred miles farther.

We reach the MSS early in the evening. It is a barn complex, and there are people around. With as much subtlety as possible, the men move the equipment inside without anybody seeing the weapons. For three hours, the gear is inspected again and the loads are distributed, MREs issued, batteries in radios replaced, and the radios checked. Then it's on the road again.

The team leader has managed to get the help of some people at a quarry site next to the Air Force installation. It is a stroke of luck or skill, because the site is not only guarded day and night, with restricted access, but the terrain has several excellent positions for our ORP. The ORP is supposed to be a secure location near the target; we make final preparations here, leave for the target from here, and meet here if we are somehow dispersed during the attack. We find the gate and the guard shack and are waved in; twenty minutes of bumpy road later, we turn off and move a hundred meters into the

trees out of sight. It is midnight. Some of us get out sleeping bags and go to sleep. The team leader stands guard. For the past ten days he has been preparing this event. He found this location for the ORP, and has made many of the preparations and arrangements. He won't sleep for another thirty hours.

At two in the morning, fifteen hours before the scheduled attack, the surveillance team is sent to take up their position overlooking the target. It is raining softly, a cold December rain, with a knife edge of chill to it. They carry with them a ladder for scaling the fence. The ladder is hidden in a small creek adjacent to the fence; if the defenders do any serious patrolling around their compound, there is a risk that it will be discovered. But this is the best, and only, cover around.

The surveillance team sets up just over the crest of a gentle hill several hundred meters from the fence, to watch and wait. It is a rather exposed position, but there is no choice. Again, if the enemy does any serious sweeps of the area, the team will probably be compromised. It's a risk. Both men flatten themselves in a shallow depression in the ground; it is full of water. They will remain there until the attack is initiated.

The plan calls for two attacks to be launched concurrently; this will spread the defenders a little thinner and help confuse them. The surveillance team is one of the attack elements. When they get the signal that the attack is initiated, they will first fire M72 LAWs at the observation towers. They'll also fire 40mm high explosive rounds from their M203s on any concentrations of troops in the area. The assault elements will all be in full MOPP 4 protective clothing, because they next fire six nerve gas grenades into the compound and pop six smoke grenades to provide some cover from any surviving defenders. Then they begin the real work of their part of the assault. They will try to capture the bomb all by themselves.

The support element is dropped off near their positions six minutes before the planned time of attack, giving them just enough time to set up while the breaching element moves toward the gate. The support element will actually initiate the attack by firing their 90mm recoilless rifles into the building where the armored cars and many of the defenders are waiting for things to happen. Exactly when they fire depends on how things go with the breaching element of the assault force. They are going to try to get through the gate with the ambulance, hopefully by ruse but by force if necessary.

The breaching element is made up of the team leader and his XO, the team sergeant, and the young lady who's come over to our side. The XO wears an Air Force captain's uniform and carries a leather briefcase. The agent has put a final coat on her makeup, giggles nervously, and hops into the cab of the vehicle. They have rehearsed their lines fifty times, in theme and variations. The assistant team leader and the agent sit up front, the team leader and team sergeant in back, both in full MOPP 4.

MOPP is one of those silly military acronyms, and stands for mission-oriented protective posture, but really means a set of clothes that includes a heavy green overall, overboots, and gas mask. MOPP Level 4 refers to that hot and sweaty condition of having all this stuff on at

the same time. As hot and sweaty as it may be, the outfit is preferable to trying to survive without it in an environment that includes the various gases and agents that the bad guys threaten to use on us. A great deal of training is currently done with the expectation of fighting in an NBC (nuclear/biological/chemical) environment, but our defenders today are not used to thinking about this kind of problem, and we may catch them flat-footed.

Much of the afternoon is spent dealing with the controllers, who have sent an emissary to find out exactly what we plan to do, so they can be prepared to evaluate both the assault and the defense of the compound. They inventory all our ammunition, just to make sure we haven't mixed in a few real grenades and 90mm recoil-

A 90mm recoilless rifle, discarded by the conventional army in favor of TOWs and Dragons, is still the weapon of choice for SF teams and Rangers.

The assault begins: The outer wire of the gate is breached; reaction vehicle approaches.

A charge is set at the door of the gate bunker.

less rounds with the artificial ones. It takes time, and as the hour for departure approaches, the team leader gets restless. There are still rehearsals and final coordination to do, and radio contact with the surveillance team is intermittent.

As the light fades, toward the end of our scheduled attack "window," we saddle up and move out, everybody jammed into the back of the ambulance. First stop is at the edge of the compound, just out of sight of the gate where the security element bails out and dashes up the berm and into the gathering night. "Have fun!" somebody calls as they depart. They will cover the assault element and take out the building with "Peacekeepers" and the reaction force with four rounds of 90mm high explosive; real 90mm HE will penetrate thirty inches of reinforced concrete and would certainly make a

mess of this building and its contents; blank 90mm HE won't penetrate anything, but it will make a flash and a bang that the controllers are supposed to recognize and take into account.

As we drive slowly toward the compound, the play unfolds. The defenders had blocked the road with a school bus, but they have removed it for some reason, and our route to the gate is wide open. This is a little present from the defenders, who have helpfully assisted us in our mission. How thoughtful! A sentry leaves the security of the guard building, where the controls for the gate are, and comes out to see who we are. He is all business until he sees our special weapon.

"Hi!" says the agent brightly. "We're here to support the exercise! Where are we supposed to park?" The sentry relaxes a little; he

The team leader and his assistant dive for cover as the fuse ignites.

''Dead'' defender lies where he was killed defending the gate.

produces a clipboard and starts to write down the vehicle ID number from the bumper; it looks like he's going to let us in. He's in no rush, though, and he doesn't seem completely confident that he is doing exactly the right thing, so the gate stays closed while he writes and talks to the agent. It is taking too long.

While this is going on, the defenders decide to test fire an M60 and set off an artillery simulator in the area where the support team is supposed to be. It seems like the signal to start the attack, and on the other side of the compound, the surveillance team starts to do their stuff. The assistant team leader gets out from behind the wheel with his briefcase to talk to the guard, who is momentarily distracted by the distant rattle of the guns and the flash and bang of the LAWs.

From the briefcase comes a Mac 10 submachine gun. The guard turns back to continue his work, looks down the muzzle of the gun, and goes into shock. A controller standing by the gate (they are all over the place), who knows what the plan is supposed to be, declares him dead—the first enemy casualty of the exercise, now fifteen seconds old.

"Let's go!" shouts the XO, and out of the back pop the team leader with the bolt cutters and the team sergeant with several LAWs. The sergeant opens the valve on the nerve gas dispenser, then climbs up on top of the vehicle and fires one of the LAWs into the Plexiglas window behind which the surviving guards watch in amazement. They are "dead" and out of the exercise, which is now about thirty seconds old.

Within seconds the fence is cut, and the team

leader and his assistant are at the door to the guard bunker; they place their charges and light the fuses. With a flash the charges explode, and the door is declared blown. The controllers open the door to reveal a few survivors in an area protected from the effects of the LAW. They are quickly killed. "Goddamn it!" one of them screams; this is not the way they thought it was going to go.

But now the fog of war descends, as it does even in notional combat: the armored cars were supposed to have been eliminated by the initial rounds from the 90mm recoilless rifle, which would have destroyed the building and all inside, but a controller didn't get the word, or didn't understand, and the vehicle is permitted to play, although by the rules of the game, it should be quite dead. The Peacekeeper brings its twin M60s to bear on the breaching team as it rolls to within fifty meters of the action, and the A team leader is declared dead at the door to the guard bunker. But the gate is now open and the ambulance rolls past the armored car, which has finally been put out of action, and down to the bunker where the bomb is stored. The surveillance team has beat them there.

The two men had gotten the ladder up, climbed over the fence, and made it to the door of the bunker before one is declared killed. The other blows the door and gets inside to the bomb before a large force of defenders (apparently immune to the effects of the gas, even though they aren't in protective clothing or masks) surrounds the place and demands his surrender. He declines and tries to negotiate. They aren't in a negotiating mood, so he puts his charges on the bomb and blows it (and himself) up.

The defenders are in full confusion. The surviving armored car dashes up to the edge of the compound and begins firing hot and heavy into a large group of its own team; they scream at the gunner to cease fire, but he fires several more long bursts at his buddies before they convince him to cut it out. They are really mad.

The controllers have had enough and call a halt to the first act of the evening's festivities.

Both teams assemble in the main building of the compound; the controllers huddle among themselves for fifteen minutes, then go off to tell the attackers and the defenders who did what to whom. They are careful not to let anybody's ego get dented. The after action review begins with the senior evaluator telling everyone: "There are no winners or losers. We

The MAC-10 is not an official part of the SF inventory, but is a popular little squirt-gun for situations where you must carry your tools in a briefcase.

all have learned something that can help us survive in combat; that makes us all winners."

The evaluation is rather gentle on the defenders, who have been well embarrassed. The assault team made mistakes, too. They will never again use a weapon to initiate an assault. They also permitted their schedule to be missed by accommodating the controller team's requests for time and attention in the hours before the scheduled attack, and missed their attack window by thirty minutes.

After this evaluation, the entire night is spent with other attacks for the benefit of the defenders. A sniper team sets up and starts to fire at the compound; a busload of reaction force personnel dash up to attack the sniper and drive right into an ambush. The entire reaction force is eliminated with several well-placed (simulated) Claymore mines.

Around sunrise, the last of the engagements is finished and both teams return to the main building to clean their weapons and equipment.

It wasn't real combat, but it will have to do.

What did we learn?

"From now on, machine gun fire will never be used to initiate anything!" says the Special Forces A team leader. "We decided on star clusters; but the other guys have star clusters, so from now on, we will initiate our attacks with *two* white star clusters, and then another two of a different color.

"That, and we need a lot more Army controllers!"

MOPP 4 gear. No, the beret is not worn, except when posing for photographers.

Learning the Drill:

Q Course

There are several criteria for joining Special Forces. The office joke is that you've got to have a Rolex watch, a star sapphire ring, and at least one divorce. You also need to get through the Q course.

A great many skills are required to execute the missions of SF, but the foundation is a program of instruction that begins in an obscure little compound in a remote and overgrown region of North Carolina about thirty-five miles northwest of Fort Bragg. The Q course (or qualification course) is the official point of entry for anyone who really wants to *deserve* to wear the beret. You can be assigned to a unit and wear the beret without graduating from the Q course, but you can't be on a team. So a lot of people wear the beret these days who are not—by the standards of tradition—qualified to put it on. There are layers of acceptance into the society and the family of SF. In a formation of an SF unit you will see many people wearing the same basic uniform and the same beret with the same flash. A few will have the SF tab, and some won't. There may be a few women standing at attention with the men, also in the same uniform, but they are not what used to be called Green Berets.

A real Green Beret is authorized to wear the tab that is awarded at the conclusion of the qualification course. Some who are authorized to wear it and all the other qualification badges, jump wings, and the rest show the ultimate

contempt by not wearing any of them. As one Green Beret says: "I don't need to wear my personnel file on my shirt." He happens to be one of the most experienced and qualified people in his unit, with some wartime experiences that would fill a book by themselves.

There is a long line of people who would like to be able to wear the tab. Unlike other Army schools, like the Basic Airborne course, the Q course is not an easy place to get into. The Army looks for two sets of criteria in an aspirant, and the first is unlike those of any other school in that it is entirely intangible and unmeasurable. The regulation says you must be: "Mature; motivated; open and humble, particularly with other races and cultures; able to display independence and authority; innovative; a team player."

Then you've got to be a male soldier, E5 to E7, a U.S. citizen, secret clearance, be Airborne qualified, a high school graduate, have a 110 GT score, be in terrific physical shape, and have at least twenty-one months left to serve.

With qualifications like these, and the blessing of your chain of command, you can stand in line and wait your turn to visit lovely Camp McKall in the picturesque rural hills of central North Carolina. Most schools in the Army are housed in rather nice buildings with all the amenities. Not the Q course. The most prestigious school in the Army is also—in terms of its physical buildings—the most primitive. Phase one is housed behind a chain link and barbed wire fence in a little compound of ragged buildings that look like they ought to be condemned by the local authorities. The buildings are old and covered with tar paper. The setting is a lot like you will find in the places where SF

Previous pages: The rappeling tower at Camp McKall looks a mile high when it's your first time down.

74

The coveted and hard-won Special Forces tab is the only real identifier for a graduate of the SF program.

The elegant and starkly modern headquarters for phase one of the SF school, Camp McKall. Behind it is the ''John Wayne Memorial Latrine.''

is supposed to work, except that these buildings are in better shape.

There is a shower; it is cold. The food is nutritious; the menu is usually an MRE for breakfast, an MRE for lunch, and an MRE for dinner. Yum!

Everything about the school is tough. A new class of about 200 men gets off the bus and is formed up at the flagpole and run up to the school compound about a mile and a half away, carrying their gear. It is the first test, and some prospective students fail even before they get through the gate. The first day is supposed to be a go/no-go test, and it is a difficult one, full of push-ups, a ruck march, and a lot of running. Welcome to charming Camp McKall! Get down and give me ten!

There are three phases to the full Q course. The first, the basic skills phase, is extremely physical. It is very demanding of a student's resolve. Discomfort is more or less a part of the instruction. Physical stress is a major part of each day in the school, because physical stress is a part of the environment where the students are supposed to work in war. There are no days off during the whole phase. You learn to run three to five miles with a rucksack. It begins weighing forty-five pounds, and by the end of the phase, it will be sixty-five. On the easy days, the run is at a fifteen-minute-mile pace. Twice a week you and your ruck have to cover a mile every eight minutes, or faster. You will train in any weather, and North Carolina can produce any weather you might want, and a lot you might object to.

All three phases take anywhere from seventeen to twenty-six weeks to complete. The medical specialty takes the longest. The first phase covers basic skills; the second teaches individual

Out of the tunnel and off through the woods, one more student staggers through the obstacle course.

specialties—weapons, communications, engineering, or medicine; the last teaches teamwork and unconventional warfare.

The attrition rate at the school is heavy, particularly in the first few days and weeks. It is often around 50 percent by the end of the first block of instruction, the twenty-seven-day non-stop basic skills phase. Sometimes it's worse. If you want to get to wear the tab, don't show up at McKall unless you are in really good shape! Another 25 to 40 percent of those who are left are eliminated during the phase two portion, and a few others are eliminated in phase three.

In the basic skills phase there is a lot of running, with and without rucksacks. There are almost daily workouts on the famed twenty-eight-station confidence course, with its instruments of torture. Most of the work on the confidence course is intended to prepare the students for the mandatory test, where they have to negotiate the mile-long course in less than thirty-five minutes.

The course of instruction includes some fundamental military skills, but they are taught and learned with a degree of intensity not found in many other schools. The land navigation training is supposed to be the best in the military (which means it's the toughest), although there are probably some Rangers who might want to argue. To get through the phase one portion of the course, you have to go crashing through the nether regions of Camp McKall to find at least three of four survey stakes that are each five kilometers apart. You are permitted to carry your full rucksack and your weapon, and you have a whole five hours to find the stakes. Didn't find them? Take more than five hours? You're a no-go. You're recycled and can start again with the next class, from the beginning. Or quit.

You learn rappelling from the tower; river crossing with poncho and rope; STABO extraction; ropes and knots; and the fine arts of patrolling, raids, and ambushes.

There is a survival field training exercise that lasts three days. You get to go camping all by yourself, with all the gear you could possibly need: a knife, a poncho, a book of matches, and (as a break from all those MREs) a rabbit. Remember to kill it before you eat it. While you're out there, you don't get to sit around and contemplate nature; you have work to do. There is a list of tasks each student is required to accomplish.

Toward the end of the cycle, the students are tested on their abilities in patrolling, raids, and ambushes. Then, it's up in a C-130 for another jump with a twelve-mile ruck march afterward, just for fun.

The survivors get to go on to phase two, which is the technical skill portion of the course. This is mostly classroom work, and it is taught in a more conventional school setting. During the second phase, students are challenged academically. The enlisted students learn their specialties: engineering, communications, medical, and weapons. The medical portion is taught mostly at Fort Sam Houston, the other courses at Bragg.

The culmination of the whole process is the

Combat jumps are a regular part of the routine for Q course students, and graduates.

cooperative teamwork required in the final phase. Here is where it all gets put together, and here is where a lot of the techniques of the UW mission are thrown at the students, hot and heavy. It all is tested in the Robin Sage exercise, which mimics a classic UW mission, including the isolation and insertion. Guerrillas are furnished, and they aren't always very cooperative, just like in the real world.

Actually, the Q course is just the beginning for SF soldiers. The whole problem of special operations is so complicated that there are

Above: Water operations are becoming increasingly important in the collection of skills expected of SF graduates. *Right:* The net climb is last on the obstacle course.

several schools that augment the foundation provided by the Q course.

One of these is the waterborne operations school, which teaches many techniques for working in and around the water. Another is the SERE school, which instructs in techniques of survival, evasion, resistance, and escape.

Still another is the HALO school, where special methods of parachute operations are the course of instruction. There is the Defense Language Institute, where the soldiers spend months becoming proficient at any of dozens of languages.

But the training never really stops. The Army is trying to be more prepared for the next conflict, small or large, and all units train hard and frequently. In the SF units in particular, there is a constant sense of preparation and rehearsal. For the challenges of the next war, the lessons of the Q course will be only a beginning.

TOOLS OF THE TRADE

The Air Force has its air-conditioned fighters, the Navy has its ships, the Army has its soldiers. The basic equipment that SF uses is first and foremost its state-of-the-art human beings. These people have been described at length already, so it might be interesting to see just what weapons and tools of the trade they use to work their magic as part of the AirLand Battle.

The whole intent of the selection and training process is to develop people who can accomplish a lot with very little. The weapons that SF expects to use are the weapons they've taken from their freshly dead enemies. The other bits and pieces of equipment, uniforms, radios, food, ammunition, and all the rest can be just about anything that will do the job. In a behind-the-lines UW environment, that may be all they will get. But in any kind of conventional combat, as in Viet Nam, the teams will

evolve ways of doing business that suit the time and place. If you happened to be on a recon team going "over the fence" in 1970 or so, here's what you'd take with you for your walk in the woods:

You'd wear "sterile" fatigues, with no identification on or in them. The uniform might be the tiger stripe camouflage pattern or the solid green OG-107 with spray-painted camouflage. Some teams wear leggings to help them move through the undergrowth, slow down leeches, and break the visual line of the leg. Instead of a beret, you'd wear a floppy jungle hat, inside of which might be sewn a part of an aircraft recognition panel for emergency use. Instead of a belt, a bandage is threaded through the belt loops; another bandage could be worn as a sweatband. Depending on the location, pants might or might not be tucked into the boot tops.

Emergency basics go into the pockets of the uniform: insect repellent; one meal; a small flare gun for signalling; six feet of nylon suspension line; maps and two notebooks with the codes, frequencies, and contact times for radio communications in the left shirt breast pocket. Attached directly to the uniform with a "dummy cord" is the signal mirror, stowed in the right pocket, along with a compass, penlight, and morphine Syrettes in their protective box.

Over this goes the load-bearing equipment (LBE), also called the web gear or combat harness. It is based on the pistol belt and suspenders, onto which you can attach an amazing collection of fashionable accessories. Although it looks a little weird, the LBE is a very effective invention. It puts a lot of essential lifesaving and life-taking equipment where you can

"FLOPPY" OR JUNGLE HAT

STEELY LOOK

STIFF UPPER LIP

LARGE "ALICE" PACK
WITH SPRAY PAINT CAMO

BIPOD FOR CAR 15

RESTRICTED
AREA
S GOVT PROPERTY
NO ADMITTANCE
AUTHORIZED
PERSONNEL ONLY

UNSTERILE UNIFORM
(NAME/INSIGNIA
SHOULD BE REMOVED)

HEARING PROTECTION

COMBAT HARNESS
"LOAD BEARING EQUIPMENT"

SLEEVES DOWN IN COMBAT

CAR 15 RIFLE

CAMOUFLAGED IN COMBAT

CANTEEN

MAGAZINE POUCH

FLASHLIGHT

GLOVES

SNIPER VEIL

83

The CAR 15 is a favorite SF weapon. It is much more temperamental than the M16 in the background.

The low crawl—one of the less difficult stations on the obstacle course.

get at it in a hurry. It lets you run with all this stuff without it flopping around too much. It distributes the weight of all the grenades, ammunition, and water so that the load is reasonably comfortable. You will not remove your LBE for the entire duration of the patrol.

The ammunition pouches go in front, where you can get at them when you need them. A bandage or bag of rice in the bottom of each pouch elevate the mags, the easier to extract them. The mags always face in the same direction so you can reload with a minimum of fumbling. On the outside of the pouches go fragmentation grenades—a minimum of four. Inspect each grenade to make sure the pin is clean and the fuse is screwed in securely. Don't

tape the handles down because when you need a grenade, you don't want to be messing around with the stupid tape.

Just outboard of the magazines, on the hips, go two canteens with a little bottle of purification tablets taped to each cap. If you keep the equipment on your pistol belt to the front, then you can lie on your back and sleep with the harness on without adding your own lumps to the ones already in the ground.

On the left suspender strap is taped a serum albumin container. With any luck you won't need it, or the morphine either. Below the container goes a snap link and Swiss seat. The snap link is attached with the gate up so you can clip yourself to the rung of a rope ladder some passing helicopter has thoughtfully lowered. This will help keep you from falling off, which is easy to do even when you haven't been wounded.

On the right suspender strap goes your knife, point up, scabbard taped down. The government hands out a rather nice fighting knife that is perfectly acceptable, but here is one of the places where personal preference is an option, and you can use a hunting knife or bayonet or whatever you think will work when you need it. Over the scabbard goes a little emergency strobe light in its container, with the opening of the pouch pointing up. This lets you operate it in the pouch to attract the attention of those friendly passing helicopters and "fast movers," while keeping both hands free to deal with the opposing team.

In your rucksack goes the things you can live without, if it comes to that: poncho, extra socks, food, pill kit, Claymore mine and booby traps, sweater, gloves, special team equipment like a camera and binoculars and any other goodies.

While the regular army uses the M16, the irregular army tends toward more exotic weapons. The CAR (Colt automatic rifle) 15 is a variation in the basic M16, but with a shorter barrel and a collapsible stock. It was originally intended for the smaller tribesmen and Vietnamese, but the teams liked it, too, and also carried it.

Another favorite weapon is thoughtfully manufactured and supplied by the Soviet Union and China, the fabled AK47. There are millions of AKs around the world, and when push comes to shove, the darn things tend to clutter up the battlefield. People just drop them here and there like they aren't interested in them anymore. You could leave them there to rust, but that would be a waste of an excellent and reliable weapon. Also, since the AK has a recognizable voice in combat, you can add an element of doubt to the opposing team when you use their own kind of weapon on them. They will have to wonder if they are firing on their own people. There are several variations on the basic AK, and they are studied in detail in the phase two portion of the Q course by the weapons specialists. They, in turn, teach the other team members and anybody else who is interested about the care and feeding of the AK.

A variety of other weapons and accessories are sometimes taken, again depending on the mission. One of these is a suppressor for the M16, and another is a silenced .22-caliber pistol. The suppressor eliminates the loud report of the M16, but since the bullet goes faster than the speed of sound, it provides its own crack.

One of the hardest stations on the obstacle course: your feet can't touch the yellow paint as you climb out, if you expect full credit.

The suppressor adds a little more confusion and uncertainty to the situation of the enemy you have just taken under fire, making it a little easier to defeat him and to accomplish your mission and survive.

The .22 pistol with its silencer is much quieter, emitting no more than a gentle little pop. The .22, however, is a gentle little projectile and not very effective at killing people, except for well-aimed shots at close range, so it is used for specialized applications. One is to disable someone you want to take prisoner, which you can do by shooting him in the right shoulder. He won't die and he won't use his weapon on you, but he'll be pretty resentful. The other basic use is to kill people at close range with a

There's no easy way to do the tunnel. Waddling is the only way to get through.

well-placed head shot. The Phoenix program used silenced .22s regularly.

Now you've got all your stuff together, and the rest of the team is waiting for you. The helicopters are inbound for the pad. You're good to go. See you in five days—if you make it back.

TIPS FROM DETACHMENT B52

Back about 1970 S. Sgt. Joe Alderman put together a collection of insights that the teams from Project DELTA acquired (the hard way) while exploring the nether regions of Southeast Asia. These lessons could only have been learned under the stress of close contact with the enemy. When the American political system decided to break contact a few years later,

the benefits of this practical experience could easily have been lost but for the preservation of these tips in a little booklet that is still handed out during the phase one part of the Q course. The following are a few selections from the booklet, which give a few clues about how the teams adapted to close combat in the jungle. They are as valid today as when they were written.

M16/CAR 15 TIPS

Use one magazine full of tracer during infiltration and exfiltration. If taken under fire, the tracers can be used to identify the enemy positions to friendly air assets.

The last three rounds in each magazine should be tracer. This reminds the firer that he needs a loaded magazine.

Always replace the cartridge in the chamber of your weapon each morning, quietly. Condensation may cause a malfunction.

During extraction do not fire weapons from helicopters after leaving the LZ; a gunship may be passing below your aircraft without your knowledge.

Do not retrieve your first expended magazine during contact because it will consume valuable time.

Place magazines upside down with the bullets pointed away from your body in the ammo pouches. This will keep dirt and water out of them, and if rounds go off due to enemy fire, you won't be injured by your own ammo.

A student struggles with ''the whopper.'' After getting up the rope, you walk the beam, cross a ladder, crawl down another rope, then dash off to another station.

89

LOAD-BEARING EQUIPMENT TIPS

Place triangular bandages in the ammo pouches. This makes it easier to remove magazines and increases the first-aid capability of your unit.

Cut the front corners of ammo pouches 1/2" to 3/4" to make it easier to remove magazines during the rainy season. Also, have two magazines with pull tabs in each pouch. If they are available, use canteen covers to carry magazines. They hold more magazines, are easier to open, and you won't need so many pouches hanging from your web gear.

All team members should carry a mixture of fragmentation, CS (tear gas), and WP (white phosphorous) grenades on their belts for the following reasons:

- Fragmentation grenades are good for inflicting casualties.
- CS grenades are ideal for stopping or slowing down enemy troops pursuing your team.
- WP grenades have a great psychological effect against enemy troops and can also be used to break contact. The use of CS and WP at the same time will more than double their effectiveness.

Smoke grenades should be carried in or on the rucksack, not on your web gear or harness. You don't fight with smoke grenades, and if you need one, 99 times out of 100 you will have time to get it from your pack.

Fold paper tape through the rings of grenades and tape the ring to the body of the grenade. The paper will tear for fast use. The tape keeps the ring open for your fingers, stops noise, and prevents snagging.

Do not carry grenades on the upper portion of your harness because the enemy will shoot at them, trying to inflict several casualties with one shot.

Always use the water from canteens in or on your rucksack before using the water in the canteens on your belt. This will insure a supply of water if you have to abandon your rucksack.

RECON PATROL TIPS

Check all team members' pockets prior to departing home base for passes, ID cards, lighters with insignias, rings with insignias, and other forms of identification. Personnel should only carry dog tags while on patrol.

The location and proper use of morphine should be known by all team members.

All survival equipment should be tied or secured to the uniform or harness to prevent loss if pockets become torn.

Each U.S. or key team member should carry maps, notebook, and SOI in the same pocket of each uniform for hasty removal by other members if one becomes a casualty.

Each team should have designated primary and alternate rally points at all times. The team leader is responsible for insuring that each team member knows the azimuth and approximate distance to each rally point or LZ.

Never take pictures of the team while on patrol. If the enemy captures the camera they will have gained invaluable intelligence.

While on patrol, move twenty minutes and halt to listen for ten minutes. Listen for half the time you move. Move and halt at irregular intervals.

Stay alert at all times. You are never 100 percent safe until you are back home.

The real thing: a BAR gunner out in the open, Viet Nam Central Highlands, circa 1969. *Don Green collection.*

aid in holding a weapon if it heats up from prolonged firing.

Avoid overconfidence—it leads to carelessness. Just because you haven't seen the enemy for 3 or 4 days doesn't mean that he isn't there or hasn't seen you.

A large percentage of patrols have been compromised due to poor noise discipline.

All personnel should camouflage faces and backs of hands in the morning, noon, and at RON or ambush positions.

Never cook or build fires on patrol. No more than two people should eat at one time. The rest of the team should be on security.

When the team stops, always check the area 40 to 60 meters in front of the perimeter.

In most areas, the enemy will send patrols along roads and major trails between the hours of 0700 and 1000 and from 1500 to 1900. Since most of the enemy's vehicular movement is at night, a team that has a road watch mission should stay no less than 200 meters from the road during the day and move up to the road just prior to last light. When the enemy makes a security check along the road, usually twice a week, he normally does not check further than 200 meters to each flank.

If the enemy is pursuing you, you should deploy delay grenades and/or Claymores of 60 to 120 seconds. In addition, throw CS grenades to your rear and flanks. Give the enemy a reason and excuse to quit.

Do not fire weapons or use Claymores if the enemy is searching for you at night. Use CS grenades instead. This will cause him to panic and will not give your position away. You can move out in relative safety while they may end up shooting each other.

Do most of your moving during the morning hours to conserve water. However, never be afraid to move at night, especially if you think your RON [remain overnight position] has been discovered.

If followed by trackers, change direction of movement often and attempt to evade or ambush your trackers. They make good POWs.

Never take your web gear off, day or night.

Gloves will protect hands from thorns and

After Action Review:

The History of UW

It is hard to know where to begin the story of this organization, whose official date of birth is only 1952. Do you go back to the American Indians, who were so skilled in the most elegant and subtle forms of fire and maneuver? Or do you go way back to ancient Egypt and the first recorded use of mercenaries about six centuries before the birth of Christ? To whom do we really owe honors and lineage?

Actually, it's hard to say. David fought an unconventional campaign against King Saul, recruiting "everyone that was in distress, and everyone that was in debt, and everyone that was discontented" (1 Samuel 22:2). Then, there was Fabius Maximus who succeeded in getting Hannibal out of Italy through harassment more than confrontation.

But we generally look to the Indian, who was a great irregular fighter. To really change history, it wouldn't have taken more than a few A teams to have helped the resistance movement that developed in America a hundred and fifty years ago. The character of the Indian fighter was just the sort of attitude SF looks for in an oppressed people, and they would have gotten things done together. This appreciation is reflected in the patch that SF adopted; it is shaped like an arrowhead, in honor of the craft and commitment of those early American patriots.

But that style of warfare just wasn't popular in the nineteenth century, when the proper way to settle disputes was to get a few hundred thousand guys together and let them bang away at each other. During the American Civil War, there were some irregular actions, mostly in the nature of small groups of raiders, usually cavalry, who prowled the flanks and rear of the enemy, seeking targets of opportunity. The whole concept was considered by the conventional forces ill-mannered and ungentlemanly. And it was, too.

Then, during World War II, most of western civilization got its butt kicked, and we very nearly lost the war to Japan and Germany. After France extinguished itself in mortal combat and the English left their guns on the beach at Dunkirk, there was just about nothing left to oppose the Nazis. German forces had gone about as far as they could go, however, and stopped to regroup and resupply before finishing off Britain.

The only thing with which the English could respond was irregular forces, which they invented in the person of the commando. The commandos were what we would call Rangers, trained and equipped for brief encounters on hostile shores. They were to raid and annoy and to put a little pressure on the bad guys. They also were supposed to collect intelligence information for the conventional forces. They existed to buy a little time, and they bought it, and paid for it in blood. They were decimated.

The official version of the SF story credits the 1st Special Service Force with being the granddaddy of SF, but there is some disagreement about that. The 1st SSF was hatched in July 1942 as a brigade of both Canadians and Americans, and was supposed to be used in a raid that would attack Norway, Italy, and Romania. After all the training, the raid was cancelled. But the troops were put to work in the Aleutians and in Italy. They were really Rangers, however, and their mandate was considerably different from what we consider UW today. So there are many who disapprove of this lineage.

The Office of Strategic Services (OSS) was formed in 1941 along the lines of the British Special Operations Executive. The OSS operations in Europe and Southeast Asia were very similar in basic ways to the contemporary missions of SF, so that parentage seems much more legitimate.

One of the foundations of the OSS was the operational groups—thirty-four-man teams that were the foundation of resistance units behind enemy lines. They trained, supplied, and coordinated the efforts of the guerrillas in Italy, Greece, Asia, Yugoslavia, and France. Then there was the fabled Jedburgh team—three-man units parachuted behind the lines to assist the resistance. The teams were composed of two officers and one enlisted radio operator. The officers were a mixed bag—some French, American, Dutch, and Belgians. More than eighty of these teams jumped into Europe. The ones that weren't caught by the Germans provided liaison with the Americans and Brits still holding out and building up on the tight little isle across the channel. Just before the invasion of France, the resistance forces got their op orders, and while the conventional forces were landing on the beaches, the unconventional forces were making a mess of the communication and transportation systems needed by the German defenders.

Although the OSS is well known for the work it did supporting the resistance in Europe, another success was less well publicized; that was in Asia, where Detachment 101 in Burma distracted the Japanese with charm and grace while Detachment 202 performed a strat recon mission behind the lines in China.

There ought to be a rule for commanders in all armies that says, "Be nice to the local folks, because if you get them mad they might come back and do nasty things to your troops." The Japanese certainly didn't follow that rule, and they got the local tribesmen in Burma well and properly annoyed. So when the troops from 101 showed up in the neighborhood, the little guys lined up to help out with the pest control project. Captain Ray Peers and 689 OSS trained and equipped and organized 10,000 tribesmen who gleefully took on the Japanese. The final body count was rather amazing: Peers and the tribesmen were able to help 10,000 Japanese achieve the honor of giving their lives for homeland and emperor, while losing only 206 of their own. General "Vinegar Joe" Stillwell came to call on Peers shortly after one successful battle, and he questioned the precision of the body. The Kachin commander produced a length of bamboo and dumped from it a huge pile of human ears before Stillwell. "Please, sir, general, divide by two," said the Kachin to the three-star accountant.

When the Japanese overran the Philippines, the American forces were faced with the choice of surrender or escape and evasion. One person who refused to surrender was Russell Volckman, who instead organized and led an effective resistance effort on Luzon. This was a true UW effort, as successful as the one in Europe, although it has never gotten as much attention. Later, Volckman was selected to help found

France, 1944: American OSS officer with French resistance fighters. OSS operations were the foundation for contemporary SF missions. *Special Warfare Museum.*

the organization we now know as Special Forces.

UW has never had many supporters in this country, so when President Roosevelt died, the OSS lost its base of support within the government. Despite the successes of the OSS, Truman had it disbanded in 1945, just when it might have done much good.

There wasn't much of any sort of army after the war. The Rangers got the ax, too, so when Korea started to bubble, the Army had to start from scratch again—as usual. General MacAr-

thur, who had forbidden any OSS activities in his Pacific theater during the recently concluded unpleasantness, was suddenly getting hammered by a bunch of guerrillas, and now he wanted to play that game, too. The only problem was that there was no preparation for a UW role. You don't pull a guerrilla force out of a hat; but MacArthur didn't care, he wanted guerrillas, and right now. He got them, but they lived short, exciting lives. The OSS would have known what to do, but they were long gone, so the troops paid for the commander's errors.

Korea saw the first actual deployment of SF people overseas, in March of 1953, but not as teams and not very effectively. About 75 soldiers were sent, most officers, few with any language skills.

The singular lack of success at guerrilla-style conflict resolution was noticed within the Army's upper levels, and a special warfare unit was infiltrated into the Army by Brig. Gen. Robert McClure, then the boss of Psychological Warfare Staff Section. Recruited for this new unit were several of the best surviving UW planners in the Army—colonels Volckman, Bank, Fertig, Waters, and McDowell—all of whom had distinguished themselves in the profession of conflict resolution. They began to develop a new doctrine and to push for a permanent UW capability.

They got a lot of opposition. Nobody, it seemed, wanted the Army to have control of UW. The Air Force, the CIA, the State Department, even the FBI wanted control, and what evolved can best be described as a goatscrew, with all of these normally dignified agencies thrashing around like a bunch of third graders in a playground fight. Truman finally intervened, and the Army got the basic UW mission while the Air Force got some crumbs. There was considerable residual ill will, a tradition maintained down the years.

Colonel Aaron Bank got command of the 10th Special Forces Group (Airborne) in April 1952 at Smoke Bomb Hill, Fort Bragg, North Carolina. The first inspections didn't take long; there were only ten men in the whole group, which was authorized about 2,500. Bank set special standards for admission to this new club: applicants had to be triple volunteers—for the Army (no draftees, please), for the Airborne (no "legs" need apply), and for SF. None could be on a first enlistment. The word got out that this was a special organization, and the men who joined began recruiting officers and NCOs they thought suitable. The result was a tremendously mixed bag of former OSS, former Rangers, former SAS, and diverse professional soldiers who had begun their careers

Unconventional forces: French resistance fighters pose with a mixed bag of weapons. *Special Warfare Museum.*

in the armies of Poland, Finland, Czechoslovakia, France, Russia, and even Germany. They were a decidedly odd lot, and that was just what was required by the time and tide of current events.

The new unit was odd in other ways. Most Army units are heavy on the youngsters, the junior enlisted people; the new SF didn't have any of them at all. Everybody who joined was either an experienced NCO or a commissioned officer, by design. They were expected to be mature, intelligent, independent, resourceful, and both physically and emotionally tough. They were expected to be able to work alone or as part of a small team, under hazardous and difficult conditions. The pattern was the old

Jedburgh team; each member had to be an extraordinary warrior and able to teach and lead others who wanted to be warriors, too.

They learned specialties as individuals and then as teams. They began to participate in exercises, and they started to use their unconventional skills against the regular Army units that opposed them; often, the OPFOR was the nearby and neighborly 82nd Airborne Division, just down the road from Smoke Bomb Hill. They played the game the way they had been taught, both behind the lines in WW II and in

American-led Burmese warriors: Detachment 101, February 1945. *Special Warfare Museum.*

the recent training—committing sabotage and infiltrating enemy territory. They used the local civilians and all the tricks of the trade that had proved so successful in France and Burma. And they worked as well against the American Army divisions as they had against the Wehrmacht. The SF guys managed to totally disrupt exercises with well-designed raids and ambushes and sabotage. Division command posts and division commanders were captured. Wheels disappeared from generals' jeeps during the night. Communications were subverted, and units were sent off on urgent missions to nowhere by authoritative voices on the radio net. Depending on your point of view, it was wonderful fun or exceedingly frustrating. The regulars popped a gasket, just like the Nazis.

In June 1953 workers in East Berlin revolted against the Soviet occupation forces and were promptly squashed. The Joint Chiefs of Staff (JCS) pondered the event and decided that the infant Special Forces were the right guys to capitalize on any future uprisings of a similar nature. They decided to ship the 10th from lovely Fort Bragg to Bad Tolz, in southern Germany. It was quite a transition. The troops went from drafty old temporary WW II buildings (which are still in use) to the luxurious and charming barracks at Flint Kaserne.

An element of the group was left at Bragg to form the nucleus for a second group, which was originally called the 77th. It took several years, but the groups developed from loud, obnoxious infant organizations to loud, even more obnoxious adolescent organizations, and began to be taken more seriously. In 1956 a small detachment of three officers and thirteen NCOs, which somebody decided to call the 14th Special Forces Operational Detachment (despite the fact that they were the first), was sent to Thailand, then to Taiwan, and finally to Viet Nam to train the troops of those nations. Another, the 8,231st, was sent to Japan. There were now about 2,000 SF troopers. The 77th had its name changed to the 7th and had about 900 believers. The 10th had 500, and the 14th was now on Okinawa with about 600 present or accounted for. It was at about this time that another oddity of this group began to get some attention—a kind of headgear as foreign to the Regular Army as the people who were beginning to wear it—the beret. That hat has a whole story of its own, so it will be saved for later.

In mid 1959 things started to get practical when the 7th sent some people to Laos for an operation called WHITE STAR, a training program typical of many operations to follow. The difference with Laos was some shooting going on in the background, and the lessons were practical, for the Laotians as well as for the Americans.

This was also the time that Jack Kennedy was getting himself infiltrated into Washington, D.C., complete with a whole new set of attitudes about government and foreign policy. He was very interested in the kinds of conflicts he saw developing around the world and became quite concerned about this country's ability to fight anything other than a full-blown version of WW III, the kind of war for which the JCS had been preparing.

American/Kachin Rangers of OSS Det. 101 cross stream on hastily constructed bridge in North Burma, December 1944. *U.S. Army.*

Lt. Wallace Welch plans an ambush operation with Kachins, OSS Detachment 101, North Burma, January 1945. *National Archives.*

Kennedy was insistent that the United States prepare for the little brushfire wars and for what he called "the long twilight struggle" of insurgencies, in thought and deed. He'd read the works of Mao, Castro, Ho, and the rest; he was a student of history and saw a vulnerability that the conventional services were generally ignoring. He looked at the arsenal of weapons and tactics and found nothing suitable for these little conflicts, except for these odd soldiers based at Fort Bragg.

He demanded that the Army develop and support SF, which it began to do with a vengeance. He demanded that equipment be developed to support the people in Asia. For example, the Americans and Laotians were being hurt by punji stakes hidden on trails. The sharp spikes were going right through the soles of the boots the troops wore. Kennedy insisted on more protective footgear, and the jungle boot with its steel sole plate was the result. It was also Kennedy who was responsible for the adoption of the M16, over the objections of some senior officers who wanted retention of the M14. The M14 was (and is) a good rifle, but it's too big for the little troops in Asia who needed an efficient weapon appropriate for their wars.

In the early '60s, the echoes of World War II

Ft. Drumm, New York, circa 1952. Early Special Forces troops huddle around a campfire. Their berets are decorated only with jump wings. *Herb Bruckner Collection/Special Warfare Museum.*

were still rumbling across Asia. The French empire was one of the casualties of the end of the war, and nationalist feelings were high among many diverse and antagonistic groups. The actions of the Soviets after the defeat of Nazi Germany created tremendous mistrust and apprehension. The Soviets, and then the Chinese, seemed to be a monolithic bloc intent on carrying on where Germany and Japan had left off. The thinking was that these nations were about to embark on a new kind of colonialism and were willing to fight dirty to get what they wanted. Little local nationalist movements got caught up in much larger global implications. So, the Viet Cong, who in some ways could be thought of as patriotic supporters of a united Viet Nam, were, from another point of view, part of a larger conspiracy.

The original idea, which died with Jack Kennedy, was that the United States would help

Viet Nam, early 1960s. An SF team pauses in the jungle. The principles learned in France in World War II were applied to SE Asia. *Dennis Mack collection.*

A tribesman from the Central Highlands, trained and led by Special Forces, examines an old VC cache of supplies. *Dennis Mack collection.*

nations under pressure to defend themselves, rather than to do the fighting for them. The Vietnamese made the case that they didn't need much help, but did need some against an exterior threat. With considerable hesitation, Kennedy's administration began to send men and materiel to Viet Nam. The armed forces of the country were, like those of many others (then and now), in a pathetic state. The original effort was strictly advisory and educational. The advisors and the mobile training teams

started with the basics and tried to develop some sense of "professionalism"—a combination of commitment, teamwork, energy, physical toughness, and skillful use of weapons and tactics.

In the Central Highlands, at the little community of Boun Enao, an experiment was tried.

105

Under fire in the landing zone, reaction force troops assault VC complex, Central Highlands, 1963.

SF-led Montagnards move into position for an ambush. *Don Green collection.*

It was pretty close to the classic UW mission, except that the SF troopers did not slip anonymously into the local woodwork as they might in Europe. Half of Detachment A113 set up shop in the small village in late 1961—eight men in an incredibly alien place, with a very difficult job. The territory was dominated by the enemy, who had tossed out the government long ago. The villagers were at the mercy of the VC.

When the people around Boun Enao found out that somebody was willing to help them fight the VC, they literally lined up at the gates of the fortified Special Forces camp. What they found was a community-based program of law

enforcement, beginning with some fundamental training. The guys from Detachment A35 handed out some war surplus weapons of diverse parentage: lots of submachine guns like the Thompson .45 caliber, the Schmisser MP40 9mm, the M3 grease gun, plus old M1 carbines and anything else that fit. These weapons were handed out in tremendous quantities to the apprentice troops, who were thrilled and honored to get them and have the chance to use them.

This was exactly what had happened in Europe and exactly what the SF planners hoped would occur in Asia. It was also an indication to the Kennedy government that there were communities within Viet Nam that would fight if given the chance. Within a year, two hundred villages were involved in self-defense under the direction of the big Americans.

During the next ten years several basic programs were developed:

CIVILIAN IRREGULAR DEFENSE GROUP: The CIDG program was the foundation of SF involvement in Viet Nam. It began in 1961 as an effort to involve the tribes of the highlands in the campaign to eliminate the VC from the central part of the country. For a variety of reasons, this force was separate from the ARVN; CIDG members were civilian employees of the U.S. Army, controlled by SF, who recruited, fed, clothed, led, and cared for them.

A Green Beret in Viet Nam. His job was to recruit, care for, and lead the tribes of the Highlands against the VC. *Don Green collection.*

109

Boun Enao was the first CIDG camp, established in 1961. Within a year there were 200 others and 12,000 irregular troopers in the CIDG. By late 1963 there were 18,000 tribesmen involved, with the support and leadership of two SF B detachments and twenty-two A teams. By 1964 there were forty camps throughout the country.

MIKE FORCE: The MIKE force was a mobile reserve and reaction force that SF could depend on when the need arose to relieve an outpost under attack. The conventional ARVN and U.S. Army and Air Force units showed themselves slow to respond to emergencies when the tribesmen were in need of help, so in 1964 a reaction force called "Eagle Flight" was developed. In 1965 a battalion-sized MIKE force was available in each corps area, plus another

CIDG (Civilian Irregular Defense Group) troopers inspect a small VC base camp, shortly before setting it afire. *Don Green collection.*

A close relationship developed between the Green Berets and the tribesmen. Here a 'Yard aidman attends to the team leader's wound. *Don Green collection.*

that could go anywhere in the country. Each was led by an A team. The little guys were all Airborne qualified, and were often solid soldiers, although they didn't do as well away from their villages as they did at home. Just the same, the MIKE forces saved the day for lots of small outposts. And when the VC and NVA were taking a few days off, the MIKE forces went looking for them in battalion-sized operations.

MOBILE GUERRILLA FORCE: By mid 1966 the MIKE strikers were feeling pretty confident, and began more exotic missions. The MGF was one of these: a company of CIDG with a recon platoon attached, led by an A team, was assigned to each of the four corps

areas of Viet Nam. Their operations involved deep penetration of enemy territory to conduct ambushes and raids. These were called Blackjack missions, and were quite successful.

COMPANY E: Once the highlands became a little more secure and a pool of fighting talent was formed, special operations became possible; they began in 1964, under the control of E Company. The first of these was Project DELTA, run by Detachment B52. (See "Tips from Detachment B52," page 88.) DELTA was the first of the long-range recon efforts to provide the conventional force commanders with accurate information from deep within enemy territory.

Projects OMEGA and SIGMA were begun in 1966 and were *really* sneaky. The CIDG troopers dressed like VC and went out to see what was cooking. They would meander down trails in enemy territory, and when they encountered an enemy force they would stop for a chat, starting with the Vietnamese version of "Say, brother, what's happening?" The troopers who survived came back with all sorts of great gossip.

GAMMA was another project, one that sent its teams into Laos, Cambodia, and occasionally into North Viet Nam.

SOG: The Studies and Observation Group was a meaningless cover name for a very large and special project that was almost entirely manned by SF, but which was not an official part of the SF routine or basic program. SOG was supposed to light a fire under the Vietnamese Special Exploitation Service, whose teams had a variety of challenging special missions. One of these missions was to penetrate North Viet Nam, which they did on several occasions. It was easier getting in alive, however, than coming back out; these missions were not often successful. But SOG was busy "across the fence" on all sides of South Viet Nam.

SOG staffers frequently led teams of indigenous troopers off for a week or so in the country; the country didn't have to be Viet Nam, either. When and if they returned, it was with some really unusual stories, a few of which are included in this chapter.

PHOENIX: A function of a guerrilla organization is that there will be leaders and officials who don't carry rifles or fight directly. They may live in villages and lead seemingly normal lives. In the late '60s, the Phoenix program targeted these people within what was left of the Viet Cong infrastructure. The information about these cadres came from many sources but resulted in a photograph of each of these persons and a little biography in a file folder somewhere in the district headquarters office.

Then, a mission was mounted against the individual. Their habits and routines were studied. When the time was right, they were "neutralized." Neutralize could mean kill, capture, or otherwise render ineffective; the latter two options were often difficult to achieve. The individuals were neutralized within the community they had dominated, as a form of psychological warfare, a message to the community that the VC were less powerful than they thought. This is one program where the

Sgt. Dennis Mack, assistant team leader, checks the map on a strike mission near the Laotian border. *Dennis Mack collection.*

Vietnamese government played a major role.

Many people in and out of SF thought Phoenix was not kosher, and now activities of this type are strongly prohibited.

During the Viet Nam War, SF soldiers were decorated with 17 Medals of Honor, 80 Distinguished Service Crosses, 765 Silver Stars, 8,369 Bronze Stars, and 2,559 Purple Hearts. Fifth Group became the most decorated unit, man for man, in the history of the Army.

It was rewarded for its valor by being deactivated, on 5 March 1971, almost immediately upon its return from Southeast Asia. Within months of the end of the U.S. combat role in the jungles of what used to be called Indochina, the lesson plans and courses of instruction dealing with counterinsurgency were eliminated from the schools run by the Army. It is a tradition of long standing that we forget the lessons of conflict at the earliest possible moment, only to have to discover them again with the next generation of soldiers.

WAR STORIES

The source of these stories is one fortyish platoon sergeant. The events he describes occurred within a twelve-month tour in the Central Highlands of Viet Nam and adjacent areas of Laos and Cambodia. He was in a program operated by the CIA but staffed mostly with Special Forces people. These missions were extremely classified at the time, and a lot of people still decline to discuss them.

The teams were combinations of tribesmen and Americans and occasionally a South Vietnam-

Two 'Yards with VC captive in remote village near the Laotian border. *Don Green collection.*

ese. There were normally two or three Americans, nine or ten tribesmen, but the total and the proportions were always subject to change. The teams were involved in observation missions, prisoner snatches, and mining the highway the NVA built to supply themselves.

A normal patrol was about five days. The team leader, usually an American NCO, received the mission; did his planning; rehearsed the team; and prepared for insertion, by helicopter, as close as tactically possible to the objective. This was normally within a five-square-kilometer (about three-square-mile) area of real estate. In the featureless jungle, it was easy to be inserted in the wrong spot—a potentially fatal error by the helicopter pilot if not discovered in time.

Once on the ground, the team instantly set up a defensive perimeter, waited, and listened. If there were enemy soldiers in the area, they would run toward the LZ—the team could hear them coming and would call for extraction. If all was quiet, the team would form up and move out, led by the "point man," and followed by the "tail gunner" security element. Movement was usually slow, and a team could spend days moving a kilometer or two.

Just before nightfall, the team would estab-

lish a secure location to sleep—the RON or "remain overnight" position. The usual way to do this was for the team leader to choose a location for the RON, but then move past it a few hundred meters. The team would sit down and appear to prepare to spend the night—in case anyone was watching. Then, just before

A RON (remain overnight) position. Sleeping bags actually were seldom used because of their bulk. *Don Green collection*.

full darkness, the team would pick up and pull back to the real RON. They would place Claymore mines all around the position and walk out past the mines to inspect the terrain, to make sure they were prepared to fight on it. Then the team set up its defensive positions, ate, and tried to sleep.

It was not unusual to be followed by the enemy, who watched and waited for a good chance to attack. The RON was a vulnerable location—if they could find it. Shifting the RON just at dusk paid off for more than one team, who had the pleasure of listening to an assault on the position they had left an hour or two earlier.

This story is about what happens when you choose the wrong RON position and fail to thoroughly check the area outside your perimeter.

STANDING GUARD FOR THE NVA

We put everyone within touching range and not one person stayed standing up. I made sure everybody was in position. But people didn't really sleep . . . you just reached out and touched them if something was going wrong. And when someone touched you, you could just feel the tension! Everybody was real keyed up, ready to fight . . . and then you could feel them just doze off again after the danger had passed.

We would put out Claymores all around. And then I'd always have the guys walk out front of the Claymore, out fifty meters past the demolitions, come back, and then everybody knew what was all around them.

I tell you one night, it was crazy! We

normally set up during twilight, well before it was dark, but that night we were late, and it was dark. And we put out the Claymores. The guys went out to look around. They probably didn't go out fifty meters like they were supposed to, and by the time they came back it was really dark.

I don't remember what time it was but it was like a herd of wild buffalos started walking through our RON. You could hear them coming, crashing through the brush, but they got right inside of our position and we were trying to be quiet. I listened to them, heard them sit down. I was cussing under my breath. I thought, I know there is a trail within fifty meters of us, and these idiots didn't see it!

Nobody on the team moved. Then I noticed the brush moving, and the interpreter came up to me. He cupped his hand around my ear, and whispered, "Chung Si, one of the North Vietnamese tells me I have guard duty next!" And I thought, MAN, THIS IS *BAD*!

I still couldn't see anybody. I thought, *What are we gonna do?* So we waited and waited. And I figured at dawn we had to do *something*. I didn't know what we were gonna do. There wasn't anything you could do. Couldn't set off the Claymores. You couldn't do anything. You just had to sit there. I was planning if it got daylight and they were still there and it started to get a little bit light, just picking up and moving out, leaving everything, Claymores and all. Just hoping that they didn't see us move out.

And, just before dawn the brush started moving again and they got up and moved out.

Sgt. Dennis Mack in front of a collapsed bunker deep in enemy territory. *Dennis Mack collection.*

And that was it. And I went, "Wow." It was close—but they moved off.

LIVE AND LET LIVE

One of the more frequent missions for the SF teams was to mine the trails the NVA trucks used at night to move supplies. The trails were heavily guarded against just the sort of direct action mission that this team was trying to accomplish. Once, on the Ho Chi Minh Trail, an NVA sentry and an SF team leader had a brief and, considering the situation, rather friendly encounter.

We were supposed to mine the Ho Chi Minh Trail, which we did on eight or ten operations.

When we go mine a trail, the team moves out like you do when you set up an ambush. When we get close to the trail the point man sees it first, and then when we move on line up to it like an ambush, with the point man at one end and the tail gunner at the other. My job, being the engineer and the team sergeant, was to set up the mine. Their job was to secure the area.

So they are watching both ends of the trail.

And I started digging. It was hard packed from all the trucks, so I am out there digging with my K Bar knife trying to break it up. I got a pretty good-sized hole and am getting ready to put in the mines when they give me the signal: *someone is coming!* I moved off the road, maybe fifteen or twenty feet in the brush.

It was a sentry who had an AK47 and he had it slung behind him, rather than in his hands. He noticed the dirt dug up, and he kept looking at it. And he looked around. He was curious, just looking around, and then he just went at a ninety degree angle from the trail, into the brush—right towards me! He never pointed his rifle or nothing, but he walked right up to me.

I had my CAR 15 in front of me. I had it pointed right at his face, no more than a few feet away. He looked at the rifle . . . and he looked at me . . . and he didn't know *what* to do! I started smiling at him, thinking, You are in *bad* trouble, buddy!

But I didn't want to shoot him. If I did, we couldn't have planted the mine. We would have had to get out of there. I wanted to plant the mine real bad.

So I didn't know what to do with him! I just figured, if he leaves, he leaves! I kind of smiled at him . . . and he let off a smile . . . and he backed up, got on the road, and kept on walking—and I just let him go.

I kept watching him. I figured he would try for his weapon, but he didn't. He did not know the other team members were covering me. As far as he was concerned there was only one person, me. I didn't know what was going through his mind—but he left!

I went back out there, finished putting in my mine, put the dirt over it, put the water over that, and we left. That night we were waiting for dusk, wondering if he reported seeing me, in which case the NVA would be looking for mines.

But about dusk you could hear the trucks fire up, just like they normally would, and going down the road. I thought, *I don't believe it!* Then the mine went off and I thought: YOU DIDN'T TELL ANYBODY! Live and let live! He just let it go; he wanted to *live!*

THE PRISONER

Unlike the pilots overhead, the artillery gunners far away, or the battalions of soldiers and Marines in the jungle, the Special Forces team did not consider the VC and NVA as a faceless evil to be destroyed at every opportunity. Occasionally, enemies would be forced together by circumstance. Once you take a prisoner, what are your personal moral obligations to the person whose life you have spared?

We were on an operation and we set up an ambush to get a prisoner. Well, we set it up on the road but they walk in columns. Quite a few columns had gone by us and we just waited.

Sure enough a column went by and a straggler was behind them and he was straggling along and the interpreter ran out there and snatched him. He had an AK47 we snatched out of his hands and drug his ass into the jungle, handcuffed and gagged him and drug him off. Everybody picked up the Claymores and moved out and we got about two or three hundred meters away and stopped and then we started questioning him.

And this guy is crying and he is really sad. I felt sorry for the guy—he was kind of wimpy and I really felt bad. We pull out his wallet and it had a couple of documents in it, but it had a picture of his family in there and I showed him the picture of his family and he told me that that was his wife and kids.

He told us that all of the time that he had gone through basic training they had told him that there are Americans on that Ho Chi Minh Trail. They mine it. They wait for you. The stragglers they pick up. That is why he was so scared. Here we were. I didn't have another American with me. I started asking him other questions, and this guy spilled his guts. He was a supply sergeant and he told me where everything was.

He couldn't read a map but he could describe it and I could pick it out on the map and I'd say, "Okay. Here and here." And I call an air strike on these places and I listen to the recon planes. They just clobbered these things. And the pilots were just ecstatic because they were getting secondary explosions. This guy told me the truth.

We kept him for two or three days in the jungle and when the helicopters came I brought him in and S2 talked to him and we didn't have no place to put these guys. He had so much information that we didn't want to give him to the Vietnamese right away. So we said, "Oh, we'll keep him."

So we kept him for three or four days and he slept in the bunker with me in my little hooch. Never had a problem. I took him over to the club and had a few beers with him and

he ate at the mess hall with us. A really nice guy!

And, then, we had to go on another operation so I give him to S2 and said, "Well, you've got to take care of him." And they say, "Okay." So they took him.

I went out on the operation and I came back and went over to S2 and I said, "Well, where is he?" "Ah, you ain't going to like this," he said, "but they give him to the Vietnamese and they took him in downtown Kontum. The Vietnamese grabbed him and they broke his arms and legs and they buried him alive."

I said, "That is *it* for prisoners! *No more!*" The next one I got after that, we let him go.

Viet Cong captive, only survivor of a VC patrol that walked into a well-prepared ambush. *Don Green collection.*

Leader's Recon:

A Commander's Thoughts

It is an interesting time for the special operations community; it is popular again, after years of neglect. The country seems to go through cycles of interest and hostility toward things military. SF has been in and out of favor two or three times; now it's the fair-haired child again, and money is no object. Money for helicopters and communications systems and any other "high-speed/low-drag" hardware imaginable is momentarily available.

The problem is that the commanders aren't really interested in the hardware. While they are being encouraged to help buy helicopters, they are really interested in getting some pack-horses and mules, some ammunition and explosives to train with, money to send the troops to language school or through the Q course or off on an FID training mission someplace where they can preach what they practice. The most sophisticated weapon an SF commander has in his inventory are his people. He scarcely needs anything else, particularly for the UW mission.

Another major issue for SF is air support from the Air Force. Many of the missions are based on the expectation of available airframes to deliver people, equipment, and weapons to staging areas and to the airspace over targets. The problem is that the Air Force often doesn't seem to be able to get it up when it's supposed to, either because of disinterest or impotence. There seems to be a lot more commitment to air combat with the sexy fighters than with what they call "ash and trash" missions in the slow C-30s and -141s. The ash and the trash, however, both belong to SF and Special Ops, who rely on transportation to accomplish their mission. The result is that about half of the scheduled air support has failed to show up for missions during the fourteen months or so that this book has been in development. It is especially hard on the reserves, who are accustomed to having their birds no-show; they are convinced that the crews simply would rather not fly on weekends and so invent problems with the birds. Without airframes, the A teams will be standing at the ramp on day one of Round Three, all dressed up with no place to go.

When a conventional unit prepares to fight the enemy, as the minutes tick away toward the time for the attack, one of the last things a combat leader will do—if he can—is to physically and personally inspect the ground over which he will lead his people and on which he will fight. It is called a leader's recon.

The battle ground for an SF commander is more treacherous. It is a global battlefield, full of natural and man-made obstacles. It is covered by the interlaced fields of fire of public opinion—foreign and domestic. Politics within the SF community, within the Army, within the government of the United States, within the world community all have an influence on the way the commander prepares to accomplish his many missions. So when SF commanders and leaders think about confronting the enemies of our country, they tend to think about a lot of things quite alien to a conventional force commander. Their recon is an intellectual and philosophical one.

Previous pages: Parachute insertion provides a reliable technique to deliver soldiers to the workplace, wherever it may be. *Right:* All dressed up with someplace to go, but not till you've been inspected by the jumpmaster.

Officers and NCOs who have made a career of Special Forces tend to preach the gospel (as they interpret it) with a particularly intense and eloquent fervor. They will do this at the drop of a hint. All of them—if they will speak to you at all—will go on for hours about the challenges, the politics, the rewards, and the hazards of a career in SF, and the role of SF in the Army and the world. The following comments come from one officer who is typical of his breed. He joined the Army at age seventeen, did an enlisted tour before going to OCS, and then went

An SF sergeant patiently endures the process of donning and adjusting parachutes and peripheral equipment, as he has done hundreds of times before.

through the Q course. At twenty-one he was a mobile advisory team leader in Viet Nam and later a district senior advisor. He's been in and out of special ops during his career, so he knows the conventional side of the house; he's been in SF for the last ten years and is now a battalion commander. He's thought about the problems of SF on a daily basis for all these

124

years and has a lot to say about the organization, its past, present, and future. This particular officer said what I've heard many of them say, almost in the same words, with the same intensity and conviction.

In this time of transition, we desperately need people who have come up through the system, who've served on an A team someplace, in positions of command, who understand the system and the issues confronting special operations and SF. We aren't getting them.

What I see as a battalion commander is a fair amount of misuse of Special Forces, a use which is very similar to Rangers. And Rangers do a very fine job at what they do; but their missions are different and distinct from what our missions are.

I don't think the Army or the military is ready to support special operations training. They say they want a special force that's capable of infiltrating behind enemy lines, organizing guer-

---

The book says you can get ten more jumpers in this C-130, but it doesn't tell you where. This is not comfortable, and when the time comes, everybody just wants out.

rilla forces, attacking targets and surviving—if necessary—for years on end, and coming out to live another day when the war is over. But in order for people to do that, they need to train in very unique ways. They need to train on foreign weapons, they need to know how to drive and even repair foreign cars. They need to know how to speak those languages, to know the customs, so that they can move around successfully in those cultures. I could not now walk around in, say, Czechoslovakia, without being noticed as being different!

If we start training for these missions the way we in Special Forces perceive that we ought to, you are going to start seeing all sorts of unusual training aides around our home station. Like pack animals, for example. They are an important form of transport in our mission area, and we are working on that, but we don't get much support from the rest of the military to do that. They look at that kind of training as part of the "cowboy" image.

One highly secret member of the special operations community of forces, primarily designed for antiterrorist missions was heavily censured for acquiring a Mercedes to use in their training. Now, I can imagine all sorts of situations where it would be important to know how to use and repair a Mercedes within the context of their missions. I don't think that we should react with such negativism to a group of people we have said need to be special.

If all they want Special Forces to do is to parachute in, attack a target and blow it up, and leave, then they don't need Special Forces! They need Rangers, they need lots of them! But the idea with Special Forces was—first and foremost—unconventional warfare: we would para-chute behind enemy lines, like the Jedburgh teams of World War II, find the resistance element, develop the resistance force and prepare it to fight the bad guys. So this little Special Forces team should be able to train a whole bunch of folks to be real good guerrilla fighters behind enemy lines! So our first role is as teachers!

Our second role is foreign internal defense, and that's what we're doing in El Salvador, and to some extent in Honduras; we're teaching countries how to defend themselves.

The third and least appropriate use of Special Forces is similar to that of Rangers, and that's strike operations, or what we sometimes call direct action missions—blowing things up, rescuing POWs, penetrating deep behind enemy lines to find out if they're really building nuclear-powered airplanes or not, things like that.

The problem now is, however, that they want to use us all on strike operations and very few of us as teachers. There is not a whole lot of support for what it takes to be a teacher in a foreign country. If I go into, say, Burma, and teach them how to defeat the bad guys in their country, I can't go in there with a lot of fancy American gear. If we're going to train them effectively, WE should be training on the equipment that THEY are using! We can't go in with our gas masks and M16s when they're using Chicom SKSs or AK47s and expect to relate to them! We have to train with them in mind.

If we are really serious about our wartime mission as it is defined, we need to train for that mission, and we aren't doing that now. Either train for the mission as defined, or redefine the mission. Do we have a need for Special Forces in our military bag of tricks, or don't we?

It is my experience in special operations that

we involve ourselves in the community of people, and the problems that confront us often have nothing to do directly with soldiering; they will have to do with the economy, with agriculture, with keeping a roof over their heads, with educating their children, with delivering babies . . . with a whole bunch of things that seem to have nothing to do with raising an army. But these are very important things to them; just training soldiers is a very narrow perspective for Special Forces training guerrillas in the art of war.

We don't really have an inventory, the way a conventional unit does. An infantry company has a motor pool with all these jeeps and trucks and tactical vehicles. Our motor pool consists of exactly one vehicle—a jeep for the commander, and I don't use it. Our inventory is our people. You can't buy them; it takes years to find and develop them to the point where they're effective.

THE CHALLENGE OF UNCONVENTIONAL THINKING WITHIN A CONVENTIONAL ARMY:

Commanding any sort of elite force is to create, to a certain extent, a group of quiet prima donnas, people with a sense of quiet self-confidence who don't need to beat on their chest in bars. When you put an A team together, and you tell them that you are going to send them on an impossible *mission and expect them to come back alive, and that they can do it, the very nature of creating a group of people like that, that thinks that way, is diametrically opposed to managing them, making them conform to a system of tight rules and regulations. It is no small wonder that, when we send them on operations we have to check and double-check to see*

that they haven't commandeered a private aircraft, or something else that will get us all in trouble. And yet, while there are those who will call Special Forces renegades and cowboys, it is the nature of the creativity that we breed into these people that causes them to be that way. And it is a constant conflict for the management of the organization to balance between creating the creative mind and keeping them within acceptable social norms. And it is no small wonder that the regular Army sometimes takes umbrage over the way we might conduct an operation.

THE LEGACY OF THE PAST AND THE MISSION TODAY:

When you look at Viet Nam in retrospect, and you look at Korea in retrospect, and you look at Central America today, in all cases we have a difficulty—because of the plurality of our politics—making a strategic *decision about the direction we want the United States to take. And the absence of the ability to make a strategic decision, the absence of the ability to declare war or to define the objectives clearly and go for them . . . causes us to do something in the gray area between win and lose. We in the Army—not just in Special Forces but senior officers in the Army—know this, we have all been to Command and General Staff College. Yet the frustrating thing is to watch us do that, to this very day, failing to get congressional support for what we're doing in Central America, so as a result, we do them in a half-baked manner that never quite gets the job done, and as a result people lose their lives for nothing.*

THE SF PHILOSOPHY:

The common denominator in most Special

Forces people is a broad perspective, a fair amount of intelligence, and a desire to do things in a smart way . . . and not in a way that is necessarily the most brawnish way. There's no question that SF people should be physically fit, but they don't fit the Rambo image. Special Forces training doesn't test brute strength as much as it tests endurance, *and the ability to still be creative, to come up with creative ways to survive, to be able to endure tremendous hardships over long periods of time. SF people would be among the last people to fix bayonets and attack a hill! They would be the first to say:* there must be a better way! *And they might apply that statement to the whole ordeal of war: there must be a better way. They look at a whole situation and say: is what we're doing here smart? Is there a better way to win the hearts and minds than with bullets? And they are as capable of applying some other way, if necessary, as they are with bullets! But they don't leap trees in a single bound, they aren't six foot five and press 380 pounds. The common denominator is a broad and creative perspective, and one that does not necessarily fit into a particular military doctrine.*

The one thing you can always count on from a Special Forces A team is a very creative approach to a problem, even if it tends to irritate a lot of folks because it is tremendously unorthodox. It is that very nature which will, I think, make us successful in war.

Afterword

The story of the Special Forces really began not with its birth in 1952 but with its first blooding in the early 1960s in the highlands of Viet Nam, where the big Americans and the little tribesmen worked together to beat the guerrillas. For ten years, that bond developed, expanded, and evolved into a very special and successful collaboration. Then, the teams were ordered out and the tribesmen and the rest of the Vietnamese were left to fend for themselves. The soldiers who had fought with the tribes felt that they were betraying a trust when they left; many were reluctant to leave. When the government of the Republic of South Viet Nam finally fell to the invading conventional forces from the north in 1975, these SF soldiers felt the betrayal was complete. It was a personal sorrow for many, and one they still talk about.

After the fall, hundreds of thousands of Vietnamese escaped to Thailand and later to refuge here in the United States. The Vietnamese escaped, but the tribesmen—who had fought so hard and faithfully alongside their American friends—were left to the dubious mercy of the forces they had been defeating for the past decade. Very few of the tribesmen got out; only several hundred did manage to escape with the thousands of Vietnamese. They were discovered recently in a camp in Thailand by several veterans of the years in the highlands. One of these was Jim Morris, former SF captain. Morris is the author of one of the best books on the Special Forces experience in the highlands, *War Story*, which is an affectionate and intense description of SF and the tribes. Morris, Don Scott from Project Concern, the Special Forces Association, and the Family Life Office of the Lutheran Church, among others, got all 220 of the tribesmen out of the camp and into the United States.

They are now settled in Greensboro, North Carolina, not far up the trail from Fort Bragg and Camp McKall, where the American side of the story began. They are all employed and doing well. They are still hardworking, cheerful, and tough. The Special Forces Association keeps an eye on them, and old SF troopers drop in to visit the Rhade and Jarai on a regular basis. Although they mostly talk about the present, nobody has forgotten the past. The bond hasn't completely broken, even after all these years. How curious and nice it is that soldiers can maintain a relationship over the decades and generations. How unlike the popular notion of the military and the Army that these people from such different cultures should still feel a sense of brotherhood and *personal commitment*. No wonder they call them Special Forces.

Appendix

THE STORY OF THE GREEN BERET

One of the special things about these SF soldiers *used to be* their headgear, and the story of the green beret is as unconventional as the rest of the force.

Back in the 1950s, when the infant organization was starting to explore the problems and potential of their mission, they spent a lot of time in the field in rural Germany and other European countries. A big part of that mission involved fitting neatly into the woodwork when and if the Red Horde decided to liberate what was left of capitalist, imperialist Europe. The beret was (and is) a standard headgear in that part of the world, for both civilians and soldiers. Berets are worn by many soldiers, including the paratroops of England and France, the French Foreign Legion, the British commandos.

There are several versions to the story of who wore the first beret. One credits two early officers, lieutenants Bruckner and Pezzelle, who are alleged to have bought black ones for the men on their team, plus an extra for Colonel Bank just in case they got caught and had to do some escape and evasion. But reliable sources at Ft. Bragg discounted that version, and indicated that it was really a guy named Don Gehb who wore the first. Gehb, now a bank president in California, says it was inspired by a movie about WW II British commandos that he and several other young NCOs watched one night. It inspired them to search the women's clothing stores in Fayetteville, where they found a green, a black, and a red beret, all of which they bought and wore on their next field problem. This was one of the first where SF began to make its reputation, and apparently one of the team was wearing a beret when he cuddled up to the sleeping general who was commanding the 82nd and whispered "you're dead" in his ear.

Teams in the field started wearing the berets when nobody was looking. It was an idea whose time had come, and people within SF continued to wear the things whenever they thought they could get away with it, with the consent and complicity of their commanders.

It was at this time that Jack Kennedy was elected president. He became extremely interested in insurgencies around the world and began asking how the United States planned to counter such efforts against friendly governments. The answer was this little group of lunatics at Bragg and Bad Tolz—the neglected stepchildren, ignored as much as possible by the regular army, who were gearing to fight a nice, big, conventional war.

Kennedy got very interested in SF. His military advisor, Maj. Gen. Chester Clifton, happened to be a friend and classmate of General Yarborough, and this advisor gave Kennedy the scoop on not only the status of SF, but the green beanie as well. JFK was fascinated with the people and the mission and the whole business with the headgear. When he went to Bragg in 1961, it was to look at the conventional and the unconventional forces that he commanded.

General Clifton recalled:

In October, when we were going to have the first Army demonstration for him, the president asked, "Are the Special Forces in it?" Finally, three days before the event, he said, "Will I see the Special Forces?" I said, "Yes, Sir, I've been down to Fort Bragg, and I have been working on it." The president said, "Will the Special Forces have green berets on?" I said, "Well, Mr. President, they don't have green berets now." His comment was, "Well, I've exercised the full authority of the presidency to put a green beret on a few troops, and it hasn't worked. Now, you know the inside of that Pentagon; you try the power of a junior officer and see if we can have those green berets on those troops. Those soldiers have this tremendous, tough job, and they need something special."

Finally, three days later, the first Special Forces man he met down there was General Yarborough, their commander. And he had a green beret on. The president said, "General Yarborough, those are very nice. How do you like the green beret?" He replied, "They're fine, sir. We've wanted them a long time. I thought they were out of supply, but when the word was passed, sir, that we could have the green beret, eight hundred of them turned up in old trunk lockers and things."

The president sort of smiled, and then he said, "Incidentally, how long have you had them?" General Yarborough got a terrified look on his face, because all the top brass of the military was looking right over the president's shoulder. He said, "Since day before yesterday, when the Army got the word that if we didn't put these on, you weren't coming to Fort Bragg."

During the war in Viet Nam, the beret quickly identified its wearer as a full-fledged member of SF, a modern samurai, a living legend, because nobody got to wear the thing who hadn't staggered all the way through the famous Q course. Until then, an aspirant wore the same silly cap as the rest of the army.

Then, the Army (in its infinite wisdom) decreed that all the people in an SF unit would wear the beret, regardless of qualification. There was considerable gnashing of teeth and sharpening of knives, but it was done. The unqualified folks, however, were required to wear a half-flash under their crest, called a candy stripe, to make sure all and sundry knew that there was an imposter lurking in the guise of a true SF soldier. The Army thought about this some more, decided the candy stripe flashes were ill advised, and it did away with them, as well. Now, everybody in a unit wears a beret, even the "leg" clerks and the women who have also been forced on the units. Many people think the significance of the beret has been diluted to the point where it is just about meaningless.

In fact, other units have gotten in on the glory. The Army Airborne wears a maroon beret; the Rangers got a black beret. But it has gotten to the point where even the gate guard at an Air Force base, whose principal qualification is that he is awake, gets to wear a beret (and some meaningless badges, too), making him look like a hard-core trooper when he isn't.

But the guys who wear the green beanie still think it has some significance and utility. Everybody has heard of the Green Berets, even if they don't really know what they do. And there is still a way to separate the real SF troop from the pretenders: the current distinction is the little tab that a Q course grad wears on his shoulder, a little patch that says "SPECIAL FORCES" in a quiet sort of way—a tab that nobody else (for the moment) can wear.

And the truth is that the beret is not even worn in the field, but is reserved for garrison and formal occasions. In any tactical situation a patrol cap or floppy jungle hat is considered proper attire, and the beret is stuffed into a pocket of your BDUs. The beret won't keep your head warm, it won't keep the sun out of your eyes, it can get you into a barroom fight, but it does have one useful application. As one old soldier says, "It makes a great airsick bag in an emergency!" But even so, it is still the most recognizable and respected headgear in the military.

THE CULT OF THE GREEN BERETS

Over the years the soldiers and the institution of Special Forces have acquired an aura that both amuses and annoys the men who wear the beret. When President Kennedy first sponsored the organization, there was a tremendous amount of media attention to the people and the institution. Media attention to the military is seldom objective, and the press romanticized this subject unmercifully. The confusion about the very name of the force goes back to the early sixties when the papers insisted on writing about the Green Berets as if that was their full and proper name.

John Wayne produced and starred in *The Green Berets*, a film that attempts to describe the work of the Special Forces in Viet Nam's highlands; it is a film that a lot of SF soldiers like. The script for the film is a pretty accurate story about camp life under the pressure of the Viet Cong. It was shot at Fort Benning, Georgia, rather than in Asia, and the quality of the acting is so poor that it detracts from the believability of the story for many people. It is full of clichés like the little orphan kid who is adopted by the A team members, but the clichés were based on fact. Every camp did seem to have a cute orphan kid who became a mascot; it is just that the film's storytelling wasn't skillful.

There were Barry Sadler's "Songs of the Green Berets" and Robin Moore's book *The Green Berets*. Moore was a very unusual case. While a civilian, he went to the Basic Airborne school at Fort Benning, then he went on to the Q course, still as a civilian—the only man to ever do so. He then went to Viet Nam and on many operations. I have a charming photograph of him holding up a dead VC like a trophy fish.

More recently, we have been blessed with a television series called "The A Team," based on the premise of an A detachment on the run in civilian life. The whole notion of renegade SF veterans is a popular one with the press and with television, and it is a notion that does the real SF individuals and the real SF institution no good at all. People believe what they see, even in these fantasies on prime-time television.

Then, of course, there's Rambo! The Rambo films are the kind of fantasy that fits neatly into the whole artificial mystique of the supermen who can violently overwhelm any enemy. These films can be entertaining, particularly if you like fantasy, but many people take them seriously, consciously and unconsciously.

News magazines insist on showing SF soldiers in the field wearing berets—even though they know that it is never done—and showing SF people doing the dramatic clichés rather than the less sensational but mission-essential jobs like teaching. This image affects the people in the units and the people who make the funding decisions. Even in combat, that image had its effect. During Viet Nam, the men on the teams knew they were expected to perform to a higher standard, because they were always in the public eye.

One old soldier recalled going to the rescue of a friend whose team was surrounded and was being killed off quickly; the team leader on the ground was on the radio, calling in air strikes

and trying to hold off the Indians until the cavalry arrived. But in the best John Wayne tradition, he kept up a running commentary on the radio for the benefit of everyone on the frequency: "It is getting dark now," his friend recalls him saying, "and it doesn't look like we can hold out much longer! We will fight to the last man! They will *not* take us alive!" He kept this stuff up for about a half hour while the air support beat up the outside of the team's perimeter and the recon team did its best to burrow into the ground. Finally they were extracted and hauled back to their camp.

"What was all that crap on the radio?" the team leader was asked by his friend.

"I have *always* wanted to do that," he replied. "Wasn't that *impressive*? If I hadn't made it back, wouldn't you have been impressed?"

His friend was impressed. Everybody was impressed. John Wayne would have been proud.

Examples of the "Green Beret cult": Sylvester Stallone's Rambo, and a Special Forces gag business card.

PHILANTHROPIST   CASUAL HERO
HERO OF THE OPPRESSED   WORLD TRAVELER

CPT. FLOYD (DOC) HAYSE

SPECIAL FORCES
FAREASTERN INDOCHINA SPECIAL FORCES
AND JUNGLE FIGHTER'S ASSOCIATION, LTD.
"KILLING IS MY BUSINESS AND
BUSINESS IS GOOD"

WARS FOUGHT	BARS EMPTIED
REVOLUTIONS STARTED	TIGERS TAMED
ASSASSINATIONS PLOTTED	COMPUTERS VERIFIED
GOVERNMENTS RUN	ORGIES ORGANIZED
UPRISINGS QUELLED	VIRGINS CONVERTED
ALLIGATOR'S CASTRATED	

About the Author/Photographer

Hans Halberstadt is a writer, photographer, and corporate film producer who sometimes lives in San Jose, California, when he is recovering from trips to Fort Bragg and Honduras. Halberstadt spent three years in the U.S. Army, which included a year in Viet Nam where he was a helicopter gunner. That experience resulted in an abiding interest in life and death issues which influences most of his projects. Previous books include USCG: ALWAYS READY, AIRBORNE: ASSAULT FROM THE SKY, and STAINED GLASS: MUSIC FOR THE EYE; soon to be released are Presidio POWER Books on the Rangers and the National Training Center.